S0-AYU-070

# CHRIST AND THE APOSTLES

# CHRIST

*and the*

# APOSTLES

*The Changing Forms of Religious Imagery*

F. M. GODFREY

THE STUDIO PUBLICATIONS · LONDON & NEW YORK

*First published 1957*

TO
DR. EDGAR SALIN

*Made in Great Britain*
*Published in London by The Studio Limited, 66 Chandos Place, WC2, and*
*in New York by The Studio Publications Inc, 432 Fourth Avenue*
*Printed and bound by Jarrold & Sons Ltd, Norwich*

## ACKNOWLEDGMENTS

The Author is indebted to Her Majesty the Queen for gracious permission to include Plate 16 from the Royal Collection at Hampton Court Palace. He also wishes to acknowledge courtesies extended by the following: The Right Hon. the Earl of Pembroke and the Right Hon. the Earl of Yarborough, Mr. C. Marshall Spink, and the late Mr. D. G. Van Beuningen, all of whom have permitted the reproduction of pictures from their collections to be included in this book. Also to:

Amsterdam, Rijksmuseum
Antwerp, Musée Royale
Assisi, Lower Church of St. Francis
Bamberg, Städtische Kunstsammlungen
Basle, Offentliche Kunstsammlung
Cortona, Museo Diocesano
Daphni Church
Detroit, Institute of Arts
Dresden, Gemälde Galerie
Florence, Carmine Church
Florence, Museo di San Marco
Florence, Museo di Sant' Apollonia
Florence, Ognissanti
Florence, Uffizi
Geneva, Musée Rath
Hamburg, Kunsthalle
Hampton Court Palace
London, Apsley House
London, National Gallery
London, Victoria and Albert Museum
London, Wallace Collection
Louvain, St. Peter's Church
Madrid, Prado
Mecheln, Church of Our Lady
Melbourne, National Gallery of Victoria
Milan, Brera
Milan, S. Maria delle Grazie
Munich, Alte Pinakothek
Naples, Museo Nazionale
Oxford, Ashmolean Museum
Oxford, Worcester College
Padua, Baptistery
Padua, Eremitani Church
Padua, Scrovegni Chapel
Palermo, Monreale Cathedral
Palermo, Palazzo Reale
Paris, Louvre
Parma, Pinacoteca
Perugia, Collegio del Cambio
Ravenna, Sant' Apollinare Nuovo
Rome, S. Luigi dei Francesi
Rome, Sistine Chapel
Rome, Vatican Museum
San Gimignano, Cathedral
Sevilla, Church of the Carità
Siena, Opera del Duomo
Urbino, Cathedral
Urbino, Ducal Palace
Venice, Academy
Venice, Correr Museum
Venice, San Trovaso
Venice, Scuola di San Rocco
Washington, D.C., Corcoran Gallery of Art
Washington, D.C., National Gallery of Art

# ILLUSTRATIONS

* *Denotes a colour plate*

# Introduction

"*Art history should deal both with the internal life of forms and with the relation of these forms to life.*" (Sir Kenneth Clark)

For more than a thousand years, from the Early Christian mosaics to the European Baroque, one of the chief concerns of the visual arts was to narrate the Life and the Passion of Christ. The Christological cycles of the Græco-Roman mosaics in Italy and in Greece created the pattern which the art of the Middle Ages and of the Early Renaissance was to follow. To watch the transformations of the Gospel story from the suggestive arabesques of the Byzantines to the full humanistic flowering of the Renaissance and after, is one of the most engaging tasks for the historian of art. So vast an iconological field had to be limited to one aspect: the life of Christ and the Apostles, and a millennium of Christian art richly reflects the changing forms and symbols of religious imagery. This it does in an autonomous language of visual presentation; and a comparative study of image-making can reveal how the Synoptic Gospels inspired successive generations of creative artists to translate into a variety of forms the vital moments of Christian history. In this power of the Christian icon to renew itself, the life of the Christian verities lay assured, and the religious experience assumes outward and visible form in the artistic creation.

. . . . .

Some of the earliest Christian mosaics at Ravenna hail from the time of Theoderic the Great, who ruled over Italy as Patricius Romanus in the name of the Eastern Emperor (493–533). At Ravenna he built himself palace and mausoleum, which vied with those of the Roman Cæsars. The oldest mosaics in his palace-church of Sant' Apollinare Nuovo, which was consecrated in 504, breathe the Roman spirit of the heroic Goth. On the north wall of the nave Christ's miracles and healings are represented, and the Christ is the youthful Olympian of Antiquity. On the southern wall the Saviour is the bearded and haggard Christ of the Passion. Discipleship is the principal theme of the cycle, and the awakening and the healing processes are contrasted on the opposite wall by acts of betrayal and defection.

Stylistically the Ravenna mosaics belong to the art of Græco-Roman classicism. The round-headed Christ with His large black eyes and long locks, foiled by the great silver wheel of the halo with the Greek cross of gold, with His frontal stance and Imperial purple, is an icon of divine majesty, but fashioned in the style of the earthly monarchs. The Apostles are clad in the senatorial toga, which is defined by simple contours and folds; but these do not enclose volume in the two-dimensional space. Hieratic solemnity is conveyed by the severity of the design, the hardness and precision of lines, the planes of purple and white upon the background of gold, the absence of all decorative detail. These Early Christian mosaics are built upon the supremacy of the human figure, with a limited range of symbolic gesture and rhythmical movement. Like Piero della Francesca's figures, they are columnar shapes in the interval of space. But they afford an incomparable insight into the world, the faith, the imagery of the Early Christians, an art of the purest existence, primitive and robust, where the word of the Scriptures is enshrined with archaic strength and directness. Whether it is the ruler of men, calling His first disciples by the lakeside, or the youthful thaumaturge, inscrutable and august, the Christ of the Ravenna mosaics always casts a spell, which men have called magic for want of a better word to express supernatural power.

Medieval Byzantine art in Italy and in Greece is far more sophisticated and Hellenistic. Otto Demus has shown how the classical order and courtly refinement of the Daphni mosaics becomes at Monreale an "agitated Baroque" and how in the churches and palaces of the Norman kings of Sicily the structural force of mosaic art is lost in effects of tapestry-like hangings and vivid dramatisation. At Daphni the Apostles are noble, elongated Alexandrine dignitaries of the court, and the composition adheres to classical calm and symmetry. Christ's followers are lofty and slender figures, great lords and ministers of their king, engaged in some courtly ritual.

The iconic power is dissipated in the mosaic decorations of Sicily, where a continuous narrative covers all the wall surfaces and vaults like an embroidered pageant upon a backcloth of gold. A processional gaiety and a courtly decorum prevail in *Christ's Entry into Jerusalem*, where the Saviour rides on His colt like an Eastern potentate, led by His chancellor (Peter) and followed by a cortège of faithful paladins. In Monreale Cathedral the classical ideal of the human figure is lost and static dignity changed into dwarfish figures with agitated limbs, embedded in "a sea of whirling drapery". In the linear style of the neo-Hellenistic tradition, with its spherical modulation of limbs, its billowing robes, the mid-Byzantine mosaic develops its drastic sense of illustration, much as Duccio, perhaps from the same source of Byzantine miniature, created his pictorial Bible for the enjoyment of illiterate people.

In no other school of painting, except perhaps the Early Venetian, is the dependence on Byzantine mosaic art so self-evident as in the School of Siena. Its greatest medieval master, Duccio di Buoninsegna, translates into panel painting the iconographical schemes and patterns of the Byzantine miniaturists and mosaics, with such identity of spirit and purpose that eminent scholars have assumed his apprenticeship with some Greek master, perhaps in Constantinople. From them he adopted the classical modes of composition, the Hellenistic types of his old men, the innuendo of symbolic gestures, the restricted concept of space and the principal colour accents of scarlet, azure and gold. Duccio's imagination was limited by the Byzantine prototypes, and the courtly style of the East. He led Byzantine painting to the threshold of the Gothic by a greater suppleness of sinuous line, by formal preciousness and elegance, by his stylish rocks and trees and architectural backgrounds. With Duccio a native element of the Sienese, an element of graphic observation enters into the painting of streets and houses, of castles, turrets and porticoes. At the eve of the Renaissance he combines dramatic intensity with classical restraint. His Byzantine types are endowed with spiritual grace and a measure of tenuous humanity. For Duccio was not only the last painter of Byzantine Antiquity, but also an ardent Christian soul, who re-created the Christian story in vivid and subtle detail, painting the Life and Passion of Christ in twenty-six separate scenes upon the back of his great altarpiece in Siena Cathedral. No other artist can rival him in the shining completeness of his narrative, which by its qualities of mass and of grouping, its facial expression and gestures—though bodies have no weight and feet do not cling—far surpasses as illustration the frozen arabesques of Byzantine art.

Yet if Duccio's world, like that of the miniaturist, is ornate, supple and intimately human, that of Giotto, who decorated the Scrovegni Chapel at Padua during the same first decade of the fourteenth century, is a Roman world of plastic relief, serenity and strength. His figures are calm and solid like the eternal rocks. Where the Sienese master works with flowing line and symbolic gesture, the Florentine is static and monumental. In Giotto the Byzantine iconography is transformed by his new realism of observation, the simple massive shapes, the telling gestures. Of him Boccaccio wrote: he translated the Greek manner of painting into Latin. His is not an art of courts and of chivalry, but of peasants and of the people. Like the Franciscan preachers he told Biblical story in its vital moments with expressive vehemence and concentration, with an eye for fact and the dramatic moment.

But the drama which Duccio conveys by agitated action is contained in the solemnity and stillness of Giotto's grave and weighty figures. For Giotto took his measure from Cavallini, who in frescoes of severe and impassive grandeur upheld the Roman style of the classical tradition. In the evolution of Italian art Giotto's cubic and space-creating shapes, in their Romanesque strength, their natural dignity reacted against the Byzantine as well as the Gothic inheritance. By his new concept of space, his amplitude of form, his graded light and his plastic colour, he anticipates Masaccio. In his epic frescoes of Christ's Passion he gave spiritual meaning to physical forms by his concentration on one dominant emotion, the balance and clarity of selective design.

The sudden outbursts of Passion-cycles during the first half of the fourteenth century came in the wake of the Franciscan movement which originated in Italy, but swept throughout Europe to the Flemish north, where Rogier van der Weyden and Dirk Bouts later became the chief protagonists of the Devozione Moderna. Giotto was stirred by the *Meditations on the Life of Christ* by Pseudo-Bonaventura which lend a new emotional emphasis to the experience of the Virgin and the disciples during the events of the Passion. The visual arts mirror the poignancy of popular religious emotion, which was kindled by the Preaching Friars and found poetic expression in the Passion Plays performed in churches, in the poems of Jacopone da Todi and the sorrowing laments of his *Stabat Mater*. The Imitation of Christ's Life, embodied by St. Francis, and the Christian Renaissance promulgated by his Order, must account for the growing demand for pictorial representations of every stage in the life of the Virgin and of Christ, which was answered by Duccio, Giotto, Orcagna and other masters of the Trecento.

Outstanding among the provincials who worked for the popular devotion in the middle of the fourteenth century are a Paduan and a Sienese painter: Giusto de' Menabuoi and Barna da Siena. They both covered large surfaces in church and baptistery with the narrative of the Gospel. Their human shapes are simple and robust, their ample robes coloured by large planes of graded reds and blues and pastel greens. Giusto's figures have something of Giotto's corporeal mass and Romanesque strength, modelled as they are by deep shadows. This Paduan master, two generations after Giotto, appears primitive and archaic, and his figures have a Byzantine uniformity of outlook, the inexpressive monotony of identical shapes. But if Giusto lacks articulation and drama, he is capable of a magnificent formalism and creates a fantastic world of his own, compounded of Romanesque shapes and an abstract landscape of symbols.

Where Giusto de' Menabuoi is placid and sober, Barna da Siena is impassioned and intensely dramatic. More than any contemporary he imparted to his large murals the agitation and the violent contrasts of the Passion plays. Like Giusto he prefers rustic shapes with credible weight of bodies and luminous robes. But where Giusto's actors are mute, those of Barna shout and gesticulate and distort their faces into violent grimaces. His is the rhetoric of the stage, equally exaggerated in mask and in movement. He modifies the Byzantine schemes of Duccio and Lorenzetti by his expressionist force and by the dramatic potential of contrasting moods. After him, the painters of Siena reverted to the flowing line and singing colours, the chivalrous art of the International Gothic with its idealised beauty of form and of raiment, which was as far removed from life as Barna's was the expression of its earthbound reality.

The greatest single advance in pictorial visualisation, which put an end to the medieval method of projecting objects upon a flat surface, came with Masaccio at the beginning of the fifteenth century. To him is due the Renaissance concept of the individual, and with it the power of endowing personal greatness with a new corporality, with real volume in the spatial illusion of depth. Masaccio peopled the real earth with a heroic race of men, clothed in antique garb. His powerful realisation of the human form, his new feeling for the receding surface of the earth on which men stand and move with massive gait, his sense for tree and descending hill, for the modelling of rounded form by means of graded colour, strong light and stark shadow, is not only an aesthetic revolution, but the pictorial equivalent of the Renaissance discovery of the world and of man, to use Burckhardt's famous formula. For the Renaissance shares with Antiquity the embodiment and even the deification of human worth and greatness in sculptural form, and a humanisation of the supernatural.

Thus Andrea Mantegna, a generation after Masaccio, is moved by a romantic nostalgia after the past, a Roman grip on reality, a marmoreal form, and even his Christian subjects are marked by a

Cæsarean spirit. His *Christ of the Agony in the Garden* is a Promethean shape, his sleeping Apostles are like fallen statues, his angels like antique genii, while his vision of the rockbound earth in the limpid air has the same crystallic harshness and bigness as his figures. In Mantegna the archæological world of ancient Rome overlaid his feeling for the living reality, and the Christian spirit is stifled in the worship of the heroic.

But so rich and so varied was the century in creative genius, that Masaccio and Mantegna lived side by side with painters in whom the propelling force was devout spirituality and religious devotion. The Dominican monk, Fra Angelico da Fiesole, decorated the cells in the Convent of San Marco during the same years that Mantegna was at work at the Eremitani frescoes. He was not only a puritanical monk, a follower of the reformed Dominican Observance, but a conventual artist of archaising tendencies. His Christ of the *Transfiguration* is painted upon gold in a mandorla of light, in the iconographical language of the Trecento. But if he disregarded the technical discoveries of his age in order to express a medieval saintliness and spirituality, he did not entirely revert to the past, and by the sureness and purity of his design, the intangible majesty of his Christ, the high seriousness and impeccable form of his sacred personages, he became the foremost religious painter of the Florentine Quattrocento.

Giovanni Bellini is the other Christian luminary of the age who freed himself from the Paduan harshness of the School of Mantegna, in order to become, like Raphael in the next century, the incomparable painter of Christian Madonnas and Sacre Conversazione. To this he brought his Venetian palette, Antonello da Messina's form-creating colour and his own sensibility for the fusion of tones with the air and the light, and a poetic vision which saw the human figure in unison with the surrounding landscape. Bellini combined with the diaphanous Venetian ambience a Grecian sense of the human form, and conceived spiritual exaltation in terms of sensual beauty. In many of his paintings the religious mood of his figures flows over into the landscape, or, perhaps nearer to the truth, the same spirit of worship inspired his painting of God's earth and all its creatures. By the plenitude of all pictorial means, the saturated colour, the matutinal light, he conceived a new beauty of man and universe, where the supernatural is clothed in the perfection of earthly raiment, an interpenetration of the Christian and the antique, which is the distinctive mark of Renaissance humanism.

In the more intellectual climate of Medicean Florence, and through the influence of a brilliant band of scholars upon the Laurentian court painters, the Florentine humanism developed in two distinct streams: Sandro Botticelli answered the classical aspirations of the Medici in mythological cycles, where his delicate and spiritual art implies a subtle glorification of his princely patrons, and Ghirlandaio who portrayed, even in the guise of religious frescoes, the contemporary life of Florence. In the secularisation of religious art which Savonarola was soon to castigate, in the sumptuous portrayal of proud princes and cultured humanists, who intrude as witnesses into Christian story, Ghirlandaio presents the worldly and decorative aspect of Quattrocento art. Aesthetically he was no innovator, and though he constructs firmly and masters grouping and aerial perspective, he preferred the static calm of placid and solid figures to expressive movement, and his religious significance is slight.

Perugino's contribution to the religious art of the Early Renaissance is more considerable. In the noble lassitude of his yearning figures, the glowing translucency of his colour, the stillness and spaciousness of his summerly skies and undulating hills, there can be felt a pantheistic oneness of man and universe, which is "the very essence of religious emotion". In the Sistine Chapel he created the classical representation of the *First Community of Apostles,* around the Christ delivering the Keys to Peter, and here the balanced grouping of firm and devoted men—portrait characters of himself and his friends—and the proportion of the human phalanx to the wide piazza, the antique temple and the limpid sky are of exhilarating perfection. If, as a religious painter, Perugino is often monotonous and sentimental, by his feeling for space and for the architectural function of the human figure, he is the forerunner of Raphael.

For it is in the works of Raphael and Leonardo that the great revolution must be traced which occurred at the turn of the sixteenth century. Now the iconographical schemes of the past, the beautiful poses and static dispositions of figures are abandoned for dramatic massing and psychological interpretation. In Leonardo's *Last Supper* the bold independence of the new age can be felt, not only in the character heads of the Apostles, the heightened expressiveness of hands and faces, the depth and tumult of their emotion, but in the dynamic force of grouping and the revolutionary freedom with which the time-hallowed conventions of the subject are discarded. In order to give an utmost physical expression to a spiritual moment and to serve his centralised architectural scheme of composition, Leonardo separated the figure of John from the side of the Lord and conjoined him in a group where he inclines his head towards a gesticulating Peter and a brooding Judas. The legend and the universal fame of the *Cenacolo* with its centrifugal groups of Apostles cannot disguise the fact that the spirit of sanctity and devotion, which inspired the older iconology of the Christian tradition, has been sacrificed and that the disciples of Christ are shown as supermen in the grip of violent conflict of the mind.

In the Roman Raphael of the Vatican Tapestries the storm and stress of Leonardo's genius has subsided, and the 'unrivalled visual imagination' of the younger artist creates in the two Christological scenes two authentical religious icons of the modern age. In both tapestries the landscape lends to the heroic figures a cosmic significance, and in both, the *Vocation* and the *Charge to Peter*, the human and the spiritual union of Christ with His disciples is the central theme. As in Masaccio's *Tribute Money*, the Apostles stand before Christ as a dedicated body of men, and in the balanced design the human form of Hellenic beauty is animated by the spirit of devoted following.

The repose of the Umbrian style, the evenness of Perugino's grouping is broken up by a variety of heightened, intensified gestures and actions. High seriousness and solemnity of the moment are conveyed by the individual response of classical figures, and each is a vital part in the rhythmical flow of the design as a whole. In Raphael's ripest style the infinity of space lends foil to dramatic movement and individual character, and the Christian legend is rendered more real by the compelling force, the spiritual ardour and the equipoise of its humanistic interpreter.

. . . . .

Northern contributions to the Apostle theme have their highlights in *Christ at the Sea of Galilee* by Konrad Witz (1444) and the Louvain *Last Supper* by Dirk Bouts (1464). Both these masters are Primitives and their respective works illustrate the Flemish inwardness of religion and the German naturalism of form. If Christ and the Apostles from Masaccio to Raphael are heroic men, dressed in antique toga or tunic, their German equivalents are troubled artisans and poor menials. Even Bouts presents the disciples as stiff and lean-bodied men with sparse beards and soulful eyes, devout, but feeble and undersized, a puritanical sect, breathing the air of the cloister. Theirs is the humble inwardness of pietistic religion, which animates the monastic art of this Flemish Primitive.

Holbein, on the other hand, in his early Passion-scenes at Basle, before his style had been formed by contact with the art of Lombardy, displays a Teutonic ruthlessness and savage realism, an almost cynical veracity of recording, which foreshadows the iconoclastic tendencies of the Reformation. These panels are perhaps not authentic. They pose the psychological problem, "how anyone could be so crude, grandiloquent and empty of original thought—and then at one leap a Holbein" (Dehio). The protagonists of Holbein's *Last Supper* and *Agony in the Garden*, where a Gothic expressionism is grafted upon elements of Grünewald and Hugo van der Goes, convey no religious sentiment, no spiritual grace, but only fierceness and intensity of the human drama, and a powerful grip on objects and figures, a strident veracity. Yet they are telling documents of northern art and of the German soul in the age of Luther.

In Italy even before the Council of Trent there was a movement afoot to reform the Church from within and to strive after a more personal relationship between God and man. The Oratorio del Divino Amore was formed in Rome under the guidance of future cardinals, such as Contarini and Sadoleto.

In contemplation and spiritual exercise they sought to reform an externalised religion, and Contarini developed a doctrine analogous to the Protestant Justification by Faith. In the sonnets which Michelangelo exchanged with Vittoria Colonna the same deepening of Christian thought and sentiment can be felt, the same ardour, the same identification with Christ's life and suffering as was practised in those aristocratic circles of the Catholic Revival. For in Ignatius Loyola a feverish enthusiasm and mystical exaltation were bound up with his soldierly ideal of obedience and conquest, and his new Order of priesthood became a rigid instrument to uphold the doctrines of the Church and to prepare its militant triumph.

In the visual arts Paolo Veronese is the pictorial equivalent of an externalised Church in whom the pomp and circumstance of secularised religion are glorified. In a Venetian pageant like the Louvre *Marriage at Cana*, the religious varnish has worn thin, and among the gorgeous silks of the guests and the gigantic musicians, we seek for long to discover Christ and His humble followers. By a complete reversal of the mosaic convention, where Christ is of superhuman shape, Veronese relegated the Saviour to the second plane, a fantastical transformation of the religious theme, where the riot of Venetian high-life amidst the Palladian palace architecture obliterates the sacred occasion. In the *Supper at Emmaus* Veronese participates in a Baroque extravaganza of devotional gestures and turns from Titian's aristocratic composure to mannerism and melodrama.

In spirit and pictorial technique Jacopo Tintoretto is his counterpart. The flame of his imagination burnt with consuming intensity. He paints religious drama with a new magic of light, a revolutionary concept of space. He has a yearning for the Infinite and breaks down the classical order of composition. He is a Venetian Byzantine, and an organiser of depth and of movement. As a religious painter of the Catholic Revival, he surrounds the Christ with mystical radiance and endows the Apostles with ecstatic fervour. His mind appears steeped in the Jesuitical precepts, that he must needs imagine the scenes of the Passion with Eastern luxuriance and paint his Christological cycles upon the walls and ceilings of the Scuola di San Rocco. He is the greatest scenic artist of the Baroque who handles his figures like the manikins with which he experimented in artificial light, rewriting sacred history in his ghostly chiaroscuro, where Christ and His saints emerge out of chaotic darkness in flashes of phosphorescent colour. His expressionism, his turbulent fantasy and his refulgence anticipate El Greco, but he is less abstract and insubstantial, closer to Michelangelo's form and to Titian's colour.

In El Greco the Spanish mystic and the memories of Byzantine symbols uprooted all conventions of representational art and created a new pictorial language for spiritual experience. El Greco found new modes of expression which, aided by Tintoretto's "handwriting of light" and by a Venetian concept of colour, have few analogies in Occidental art. He invented his own forms, his own scale of figures, his own substance and density of objects, his own movement, light and physiognomical shapes. From them he compounded the pictorial equivalent of spiritual bodies, the celestial hierarchy, the experience of mystical elevation. In such a world of religious fantasy, gravity and perspective are of no account, and the elongated supernatural forms with their trance-like expression are liberated from all optical laws, as are the amorphous shapes of cloud and rock, the spiral draperies, the distorted limbs and faces. The concentrated emotion of a mystical luminary cannot be contained in static bodies, and El Greco's shapes have the flickering, swirling substance of fire.

After El Greco—the earthiness, the essential sanity of Rubens not only illustrate a difference in spiritual temper, but that between the Spanish and the Flemish Baroque. In Rubens even the figure of the Resurrected Christ has the radiant beauty of a splendid nude, and in his paintings like the *Charge to Peter* or the *Incredulity of Thomas*, the Christ fills half the picture-space, and by His physical presence balances alone the three or four figures opposite. In the *Last Supper* and *Emmaus* pictures the unifying force is the light, the mysterious candle-light of the one, the deep sunset glow of the other. Here as elsewhere the central position of Christ is abandoned. The Baroque has other means of accent and spiritual emphasis, and in the high-poetical *Supper at Emmaus*, the centre is left free for a landscape of architecture and rolling countryside. But above all it is the warmth and generous humanity of Rubens which lend to his presentations of sacred story their vitality and distinction, and Burckhardt thought that something of his own personality had entered into "the Christ of consolation and succour".

To confront Rubens with Rembrandt is to step from the joyful and radiant paganism of the southern Netherlands into the puritanical gloom of Holland. In Rubens' *Emmaus* picture the mysticism, the effusion of love and of worship are Catholic, embracing and beautifying nature and man. Rembrandt's tragic Christ is an emanation of the Protestant spirit, sorrowful, ghostly, severe, a tortured and resurrected God, the Son of Man, yet by His magical raiment transcending into the realm of the supernatural—an image of the inward-looking, self-denying Protestant soul. If Rubens emphasises the worldly aspect, the humanity of Christ, Rembrandt's "divine revenant" expresses the otherness of the apparition. Of the Baroque nothing remains but the powerful vaulted niche where the three are ensconced. Rembrandt's realistic veracity fathoms the Crucified in the paucity of His body, the abnegation of the flesh, the "lowliness, pathos and solemnity" with which he conceived the Christian epic.

Religious painting in the eighteenth century shows the festive exuberance and flamboyancy of the Rococo style, triumphant in Tiepolo and a host of smaller masters, whose art was kindled by his exultant pictorial music. Tiepolo, by his fascination with light and its "iridescent splendour", by his aerial fantasies and the dramatic pathos of his stage-designs, applied equally to heathen mythologies and to scenes from Christ's Passion, by his illusionistic power and the fusion of Palladian architecture with Venetian skies, has been called a Veronese Redivivus. In him neo-classical elements blend with the elegance, grace and melodrama of the Rococo. This eighteenth-century art reflects a light-hearted and optimistic religion, a jubilant symphony, comparable to the passionate cadences of Mozartian music. If it is essentially decorative art and at times operatic and sentimental, if shapes and rhythms seem to dissolve into aerial nothing, as in a celestial ballet, it must yet be accounted among the last authentic voices which can be heard in the religious art of the Western world.

. . . . .

The historian of art examines the changing forms of aesthetic expression in the context of their historical background, and reads the monuments as an unerring documentary of the spirit of the age and of their individual makers. The following plates will reveal what vital changes of stylistic treatment the iconography of Christ's life with the Apostles undergoes in twelve centuries of artistic creation. Each authentic work of art, from the archaic strength of the mosaics to the medieval symbolism of Duccio, from Masaccio's powerful humanity to the grandeur of the High Renaissance, from the tender sentimentality of the Baroque to the tragic depth of Rembrandt, follows its own formal laws of expression and reflects the religious sensibilities of the time. Thus the continuity of religious beliefs, shattered by the Reformation, is also reflected in sacred art, and the barrenness of Protestant churches was opposed by a new efflorescence of Catholic picture-making. The Council of Trent condemned what the Popes of the Renaissance condoned. Henceforth the Jesuit Order and the Holy Office watched over the work of their painters and compelled them to avoid "erroneous doctrine" and impurity in art. "In a few years," wrote Emile Mâle in his *L'Art Religieux après le Concile de Trente*, "the spirit of the Church was fundamentally changed." Art had to be restrained and noble, and the Church rejected the worldiness of Veronese, and Caravaggio's veracity. It enlisted great artists as well as powerful men of letters to uphold its doctrine against the Protestant onslaught. "To the Protestants who wanted to contemplate Christ only in the spirit, the Church replies by multiplying images." Emile Mâle has shown the impact of the Catholic Revival upon the painting of the Last Supper, and how the Institution of the Eucharist took precedence over the announcement of the Betrayal. In paintings by Ribera and Barocci, by Poussin and Rubens, the Last Supper appears "like a Mass celebrated by Christ". Thus the great religious conflict of the seventeenth century is reflected in the visual arts, which are "the most trustworthy" self-expression in the life of nations.

# I. *The Calling of the Apostles*

"*Now as he walked by the Sea of Galilee, he saw Simon, and Andrew his brother, casting a net into the Sea (for they were fishers.) And Jesus said unto them, Come ye after me; and I will make you to become fishers of men. And straightway they forsook their nets, and followed him. And when he had gone a little further thence, he saw James the son of Zebedee, and John his brother, who also were in the ship mending their nets. And straightway he called them: and they left their father Zebedee in the ship with the hired servants, and went after him.*" (Mark i, 16–20)

PLATE I
MOSAIC,
SIXTH CENTURY,
RAVENNA

Christ's first social act is the calling of disciples and the creation of a new human and spiritual order. The master of the sixth-century mosaics at Ravenna commemorated the scene in a design of archaic simplicity. The beardless and Apollo-like Christ, His Roman head with the rich crown of hair foiled by the large cross-nimbus, stands out in solitary grandeur from the background of gold. He is clad in the Imperial purple, and His frontal stance, His magical gaze enhance His majestic appearance. He has raised His right hand in a gesture of beckoning as well as blessing, and this connects His figure with the two disciples in the boat, who have cast their net into the azure sea, where a dolphin gambols over the waves. A mysterious companion in a white toga, standing behind Christ, strengthens His action by his presence and pointing hand. The mosaicist has built his design upon the contrast between the commanding figure of Christ, upright in the near foreground, and the stooping posture of the Apostles Peter and Andrew, in whom are expressed the dawning faith, awe and devotion. Within the limitations of the medium, where the frontality of all figures and the resplendent gold preclude the third dimension, the Ravenna master created the hieratic pattern which profoundly influenced medieval mosaicists and painters. Duccio and also Giotto work in the Byzantine tradition, and Duccio's *Calling of the Apostles Peter and Andrew* is all but identical with the Ravenna mosaic.

PLATE 2
DUCCIO DI
BUONINSEGNA

The style of Duccio is that of the miniaturist. But though the iconography is borrowed, the Roman strength of the Ravenna mosaic has become Gothicised and refined. The supernatural is humanised and the Apostles with their "heavy lips and wrinkles of a Socratic kind", their Hellenistic hair and beards, have a touching humility. Andrew hears but does not comprehend; but Peter, stout-hearted and sturdy, raises his hand as if to swear allegiance, and gazes at the Christ in eagerness of dedication. Yet if the Apostles, the greenish-blue sea, the golden foil are quite literal translations of mosaic art into panel painting, the finesse of the miniaturist's brush employs a deeper *colorito*, a more sinuous and mobile line and a formal elegance, especially in the slender figure of Christ, who in His luminous red and blue robes stands on the narrow cliff, with fixed gaze and bidding hand, calling His first disciples.

PLATE 3
GIUSTO DE'
MENABUOI

With Giusto de' Menabuoi, a Paduan painter of the Late Trecento, the Byzantine scheme begins to be modified. Peter and Andrew in robes of white and of gold have left the boat in an impetuous movement and thrown themselves at the feet of Christ. Upon the bluish-black Sea of Galilee, bounded by fantastical rocks, the sons of Zebedee with their father approach in another boat. The turbulent water, stretching almost to the line of the horizon, is suggested by the curling spirals of waves. There is something grandly primitive in this ghostly landscape of Menabuoi's fresco upon the walls of the Paduan Baptistery and in the monumental figures in ample robes of graded colour, boldly modelled in the light. Romanesque strength and solidity of the figures are contrasted by the barren peaks, the tiny boats tossing upon the sea, inscribed with a total disregard for perspective and for the plastic relationship of figures and objects in the surrounding space. For this is an abstract landscape, bearing small resemblance to reality, a landscape of symbols, with its square expanse of water and the minute profile of a medieval town tucked away in the corner.

Half a century later, in the same city of Padua, the youthful Mantegna painted the *Calling of James and John* upon the walls of the Eremitani Church; and here, in front of the compact design, the heroic vision of nature into which the human act of the foreground is laid, one feels at once the presence of a great master. The miracle is that the human group is not dwarfed by the towering rock formations, piled up heavenwards, layer upon layer, like some gigantic cathedral of nature. The Christ who with strength and dignity urges the sons of Zebedee to become His followers, the heroic shapes of Peter and Andrew by His side, the kneeling disciples yearning to accept His call, even the old hunched-up fisherman in the boat—their Roman statures, their sculptured bodies, their metallic folds have the same firmness and rigid contours as the "stratified" rocks. The distant pile of the man-made castle, the sunrise sky with the flight of birds, the barren foreground of rock and pebble complete Mantegna's vision of the primeval earth, where on the morning of history Christ chooses His first companions.

PLATE 4
ANDREA
MANTEGNA

Then at the height of the Renaissance Domenico Ghirlandaio painted the *Calling of Peter and Andrew* in the Sistine Chapel at Rome, a great pageant picture of many figures in an enchanting landscape of receding hills and sunlit water. In the middle distance Christ addresses the fishermen in their boat, but in the near foreground the disciples kneel before their Master, surrounded by a multitude of Florentine men and youths, in splendid period costumes, indispensable to the Medicean court painter. The human significance, where Christ on the lonely shore comes upon His first followers, is weakened by this grand display of irrelevant figures, this classical composition with its balanced grouping and symmetry. And though the Saviour is a noble human form, the Apostles seem bare of expression and emotion, performers of a rite, actors in a pageant, where onlookers and scenic backdrops and the chief protagonists have the same pictorial values.

PLATE 5
DOMENICO
GHIRLANDAIO

Close on the *Calling of Peter and Andrew* in St. Mark's Gospel follows the *Vocation of the Sons of Zebedee*. Christ's magical power to call into His allegiance the simple fishermen from the Sea of Galilee has been fully grasped and rendered in two paintings of about 1510 by Marco Basaiti, a follower of Giovanni Bellini. The encounter takes place before a Venetian landscape of great beauty. Here, before a vast prospect of limpid water and sunlit air and receding blue mountains, divided in the middle distance by a rocky escarpment with a walled city, Christ between Andrew and Peter blesses the new disciples whom He has chosen. In the mysterious half-smile of love to which the sons of Zebedee respond by their eager devotion, James upon his knees with a gesture of self-dedication, John walking with winged step towards the Master and pointing to his father in the boat—Basaiti has rendered the tension of the scene and painted the most humanly direct and appealing of all vocations. For though his figures are a little lean and angular, he has a full command over light and aerial atmosphere and graded colour, and the human mystery flows over into the landscape, the misty blue of air and alpine ranges, where a pale golden light unifies and embraces all. Basaiti rendered the vital moment of the awakening, the spark which kindles the fire of a new life in the Apostles and the supernatural aura which surrounds the Christ.

PLATE 6
MARCO
BASAITI

"*And he went forth again by the sea side, and all the multitude resorted unto him, and he taught them. And as he passed by, he saw Levi the son of Alphæus sitting at the receipt of custom, and said unto him, Follow me. And he arose, and followed him.*" (Mark ii, 13–14)

In 1598 Caravaggio painted in Rome the *Calling of Matthew* in the Venetian style and with a strong emphasis on dramatic light. The beam that floods the back wall and the inmates of the gamblers' den, leaves Christ in semi-darkness, whose commanding hand points towards Matthew sitting at the custom's

PLATE 7
MICHELANGELO
MERISI DA
CARAVAGGIO

table. The Apostle who accompanies Christ to the disreputable place, where the young gallants in doublet and sword and feathered hat spread the atmosphere of the guardroom, almost obliterates Christ's figure and repeats His gesture. Matthew in dark velvet dress and beret and in the pallor of his refined features gazes at the Christ with the shock of seeing a phantom. Two of the gamblers remain unaware of the visitants from another world; and though the mystical contact between the Saviour and the Apostle is established, the religious significance of the scene is obscured by the stark realism of Caravaggio, his irreverent reading of the Scriptures.

The diagonal shaft of light which hits the face of the pretty youth by the side of Matthew, the still-life of purse, inkwell and book upon the table, the ruffian engrossed in counting his gain, and the vulgar companion who has veered around on his chair, are elements of Caravaggio's naturalistic daring. For the contrast between the toga-clad and barefoot emissaries of the other world with the modern dress of the young officers, is as striking as that between the half-light in which Christ and the Apostles are shrouded and the glare upon the publicans' faces. Nor are the countenance and gesture of Christ without an ascetic and mystical urgency, which kindles in Matthew the fire of comprehension and a desire for regeneration. Yet Caravaggio, by his fascination with light and chiaroscuro, and by his love of painting these Roman youths in Venetian garb, transformed the sacred subject into a painting of genre.

# II. *The Miraculous Draught of Fishes*

*"Now when he had left speaking, he said unto Simon, Launch out into the deep, and let down your nets for a draught. And Simon answering, said unto him, Master, we have toiled all the night, and have taken nothing: nevertheless at thy word I will let down the net. And when they had this done, they inclosed a great multitude of fishes, and their net brake: And they beckoned unto their partners, which were in the other ship, that they should come and help them. And they came, and filled both the ships, so that they began to sink. When Simon Peter saw it, he fell down at Jesus' knees, saying, Depart from me, for I am a sinful man, O Lord."* (Luke v, 4–8)

PLATE 8
DUCCIO DI BUONINSEGNA

Duccio's rendering of the scene is impressive by its human momentum, the reflection of awe in the fishermen's faces, the varied grouping where three of them with gestures perhaps more symbolic than real, haul in the fish, while their companions gaze over their shoulders towards the Christ. Peter has left the boat and, straining to come to Christ on the near-by shore, with fixed and ardent gaze and arms eager to embrace, links the men in the boat with the dark solitary figure in His gold-streaked mantle. All this is suggested by the innuendo of gestures, the arabesque of movements, within the conventions of the Byzantine pattern, yet made more persuasive by the supple forms and contours, the contrast of rich and radiant colours, like the pale blue and bright red of the Apostles' tunics. But, above all, it is the beauty and balance of the design as a whole, the simple arabesque of the boat with the group of startled fishermen, and the plastic illusion in depth, which mark the picture as one of the boldest of the series. Only the heads of the Apostles with their bulging craniums and Byzantine highlights are still the traditional types of medieval mosaics.

PLATE 9
RAPHAEL

Two centuries after Duccio, at the apex of the Renaissance under Pope Leo X, Raphael designed for the Sistine Chapel the world-famous tapestry with scenes from the lives of the Apostles Peter and Paul. The cartoon for the *Miraculous Draught of Fishes* was completed in 1517. The two boats are small and flat so that the human figures and actions come into full relief before the wide expanse of tranquil water under the high horizon. Peter has thrown himself on his knees in fervent worship amidst the abundance of fish, and Christ at the helm calms the excited man. But the central figure of the composition is Andrew standing in the boat, his hair ruffled by the wind, making an eloquent gesture of wonder and adoration.

The amazement at the stupendous catch, the gratitude and devotion are divided between these two powerful figures, and the emotional impact is strengthened by this division. Composed and dignified, the heroic figures move freely in the surrounding air. Duccio's fishermen hauling in the net have now become two Michelangelesque half-nudes, straining their muscular backs and arms, while hair and drapery flutter in the breeze. Even the herons in the foreground mirror the agitation in the boat and the undulating shore re-echoes the rising and falling lines of the sculptural figures. In the architectural build-up of the scene, the rhythmical movement of Peter and Andrew towards the Christ is perfectly balanced by the two straining youths in the second boat, and the composition as a whole "seems full of repose". As Wölfflin wrote in his *Classic Art*, Raphael's *Miraculous Draught*, like Leonardo's *Last Supper*, is one of those works "which cannot henceforth be conceived otherwise".

PLATE 10
PETER PAUL
RUBENS

Yet one later artist at least ventured on the impossible task, Rubens, who painted for the Church of Our Lady at Mecheln a *Miraculous Draught of Fishes*, which is as far removed from the classical harmony and composure of Raphael as an artist of the Flemish Baroque is wont to be. The religious significance of the scene is now confined to a traditional Christ, silhouetted in His dark red robe against the blue sky, standing in the boat and comforting Peter. As the Apostle kneels and renders thanks in his humility, he presses his blue sailor's cap against his naked breast, a gigantic and touching shape, separated from the rest of the company. For Rubens used the religious subject as a mere pretext for this tremendous fishing scene, with its splendid anatomies in movement, its tempestuous orchestration of reds and sea-green and shining flesh tints, its strains and stresses of physical exertions and its fantastical holocaust of wriggling and glaring fish.

No effort of the imagination can endow these Flemish fishermen, tugging at their net, with apostolic saintliness; neither the flaxen-haired Norseman in his great sea-boots and red jacket, nor the bare and bearded rustics by his side. But we can study the Baroque laws of composition, the substitution of classical order and restraint by a whirl of movement and counter-movement, by diagonal recession in depth and by vitalising, composite colour.

# III. *The Marriage at Cana*

"*And the third day there was a marriage in Cana of Galilee, and the mother of Jesus was there. And both Jesus was called, and his disciples, to the marriage. And when they wanted wine, the mother of Jesus saith unto him, They have no wine. Jesus saith unto her, Woman, what have I to do with thee? mine hour is not yet come. His mother saith unto the servants, Whatsoever he saith unto you, do it. And there were set there six waterpots of stone, after the manner of the purifying of the Jews, containing two or three firkins apiece. Jesus saith unto them, Fill the waterpots with water. And they filled them up to the brim. And he saith unto them, Draw out now, and bear unto the governor of the feast. And they bare it. When the ruler of the feast had tasted the water that was made wine, and knew not whence it was, (but the servants which drew the water knew) the governor of the feast called the bridegroom. And saith unto him, Every man at the beginning doth set forth good wine, and when men have well drunk, then that which is worse: but thou hast kept the good wine until now. This beginning of miracles did Jesus in Cana of Galilee, and manifested forth his glory, and his disciples believed on him.*" (John ii, 1–11)

PLATE 11 MOSAIC, SIXTH CENTURY, RAVENNA

Perhaps no other Biblical scene spans such a variety of pictorial interpretation, from the sparing language of symbols of the Ravenna mosaic to the full blast of Veronese's Venetian banquet. In Sant' Apollinare Nuovo the magical act of Christ in turning water to wine is related by a group of three figures: Christ in His purple toga stands by the side of the vessels in frontal position, His hands held downward over the water in an act of blessing or incantation. The white-robed companion in the centre is the solemn witness of the miracle, the open palm of his right hand raised in wonder. To the left a servant gazes at Christ in eagerness and stupor. There is a sense of geometrical pattern in the pyramid of the group, the diagonal of folds, and the measured action of Christ is met by the impetuous forward thrust of the servant. Between these two figures the pillar-like companion of Christ enhances the solemnity of the miracle. For it is the miracle, not the feast, which the mosaicist has presented in the concentrated shorthand of his art.

Duccio, with his limited means of giving substance to bodies and credible movement, aimed at a more detailed representation of the scene. In the unreal space and perspective the disproportionate bodies twist and bend, illustrating the story by suggestion and symbol.

PLATE 12 GIOTTO DI BONDONE

Giotto in the Scrovegni Chapel brings order into the chaos and invests Duccio's shadows with weight and gravity. Here beneath a wooden canopy which tops the walls of an open hall, the company is seated behind the table. It is not only the conspicuous form of the pot-bellied cellarer in a rose-pink tunic, or the Roman jars on the bench, which belong to an objective world within recognisable space, but also the dignified principals at the table: the noble Christ addressing the simple peasant girl, or the solemn bride, her dark red robe contrasted by the Virgin's blue. Giotto's Christ is still the bearer of Byzantine majesty, virile, commanding, with dark hair and beard. The story is told in the restrained language of weighty figures, well spaced, with sparing gestures and grave looks, and here and there the realist's contempt for beauty of the human form.

PLATE 13 GIUSTO DE' MENABUOI

Or we may turn to another Paduan picture of the Marriage Feast by a late-comer in the following of Giotto, Giusto de' Menabuoi. He also adopted the L-shaped table, but it is larger and the grouping is not adumbrated by foreground figures. Giotto's balcony has now grown into a rectangular loggia with Romanesque arches and considerable depth of recession. The apostolic figures and guests are not of marked individuality in themselves, they are typified in the Byzantine fashion with their gleaming almond-shaped eyes, but they have corporeal mass and are richly modelled by shadow. Christ at the head of the table in a luminous blue mantle beckons to the servants. His gesture seems undecisive, between blessing and instructing. Yet the servants, stout and undersized Roman shapes, flock towards Him in adoration—for "the servants which drew the water knew"—and one of them fills the ornamental jars, while the governor of the feast samples the wine. Giusto's rendering of the scene, though a little heavy in bulk and conventional in gesture, combines the stereotyped Byzantine scale of expression with a Romanesque sense of form, and on the lower plane, where the servants move amidst the long-necked bottles, he proves himself an artist of original fantasy and vision.

PLATE 14
PAOLO
VERONESE

The miracle of the wine is overshadowed by Veronese's Venetian pageant; the religious varnish wears thin and the Christ is eclipsed by the gigantic musicians in the foreground and their gorgeous silks. Earlier, more devotional ages, had distinguished the holy personages by painting them larger than the rest of humanity. The Pantocrator of the mosaics is of supernatural height and hieratic dignity. Veronese's Christ—though His head is radiant and His gaze magically transfixed, though a small inner circle is aware of the miracle and turns towards Him in marked amazement—is relegated to the second plane between the cooks' gallery and the proscenium of the musicians, and the miracle is hidden from the festive assembly.

Yet it remains the most fantastical transformation of the theme, a landmark in the secularisation of religious art; and if the miracle is obscured, the Marriage Feast has its full sway in the organisation of huge decorative surfaces. The Palladian architecture of classical columns and friezes, flooded by light and seen against the blue infinity of the sky, lends a perspective frame to the crowded canvas. In it, sumptuousness reigns without being gaudy, postures are varied without monotony, a generous sweep of robes, a surging sea of figures, Lords of the Serenissima in all their finery of Venetian reds and silvery whites—these are the elements of the *tableau vivant*, a riot of opalescent colour and composite tones, a total metamorphosis of the patriarchal feast into the outward splendour, the material luxuriance of Renaissance Venice.

# IV. *The Sending Out of the Apostles*

*"Then he called his twelve disciples together, and gave them power and authority over all devils, and to cure diseases. And he sent them to preach the Kingdom of God, and to heal the sick. And he said unto them, Take nothing for your journey, neither staves, nor scrip, neither bread, neither money, neither have two coats apiece. And whatsoever house ye enter into, there abide, and thence depart. And whosoever will not receive you, when ye go out of that city, shake off the very dust from your feet for a testimony against them. And they departed, and went through the towns, preaching the Gospel, and healing every where."* (Luke ix, 1–6)

PLATE 15
A SOUTH
GERMAN
MASTER

The sending out of the Apostles is a rare subject in the iconography of religious art. But a South German master of the sixteenth century represented the very act of the Apostles' departure, before a topographical landscape of Bamberg. Here the Apostles set out on their journey two by two, barefoot, with their staves and quaint hats, with brotherly embrace and a last word of parting. The artist has painted three foreground groups of large figures, standing by the rivulet where one of them fills his bottle amidst the dainty plants and pebbles, bearded pilgrims, pious monks and a youth who arrests by his earnest and pensive beauty. Others in the middle distance are already wending their way among the spiky rocks towards the proud medieval town with its walls and turrets and many spires and the great cathedral, nestling in the saddle between the Franconian Hills. The homely Apostles, simple folk of cobblers and carpenters, with large heads and soulful glances, men of character and experience, filled with religious ardour, ecstatic messengers of the faith, recall the Apostles around the deathbed of Mary by Hugo van der Goes. The Bamberg master must have been acquainted with the art of the Netherlands. The graphic clarity of the city landscape, the build-up of serried houses in the limpid air of the south, the river with toll-gate and bridge, the tree-dotted hills, are of Flemish descent. But above all he has expressed the spirit which links the Apostles in a new bond of Christian brotherhood.

PLATE 16
HANS HOLBEIN
THE YOUNGER

Another rendering of the Apostles' obedience towards Christ's command, to go into the world and preach the kingdom of God, can be found in the background of Holbein's *Noli Me Tangere*. Here between the Resurrected Christ who recoils from Magdalena, before a wide sweeping valley of the Jura Mountains, Peter strides out, barelegged, leaning on his staff, impatient, irascible, acknowledging as he walks the leadership of John. Holbein has set down the swiftness of the Apostles' gait, the great strides, the fluttering robes, the daring silhouettes, seen against the panorama of the world into which they are passing. Perhaps it is Holbein's interpretation of the mystery contained in Christ's parting words to Peter in the last chapter of the Fourth Gospel: "If I will that he tarry till I come, what is that to thee? Follow thou me." Thus in Holbein's group the youthful John leads the Apostle towards his fate, who, because the Lord so ordained it, follows ungrudgingly, bowing his wintry head.

# V. *The Miracle of the Loaves and Fishes*

"*And when it was evening, his Disciples came to him, saying, This is a desert place, and the time is now past; send the multitude away, that they may go into the villages, and buy themselves victuals. But Jesus said unto them, They need not depart; give ye them to eat. And they say unto him, We have here but five loaves, and two fishes. He said, Bring them hither to me. And he commanded the multitude to sit down on the grass, and took the five loaves, and the two fishes, and looking up to heaven, he blessed, and brake, and gave the loaves to his Disciples, and the Disciples to the multitude. And they did all eat, and were filled: and they took up of the fragments that remained twelve baskets full. And they that had eaten were about five thousand men, beside women and children.*"
(Matthew xiv, 15–21)

PLATE 17
MOSAIC,
SIXTH CENTURY,
RAVENNA

The Feeding of the Five Thousand is no easy subject for representational art. But the master of the Ravenna mosaics possessed a keen sense of the essential and had no compunction about pruning the story and rendering only the heart of the matter: the blessing of the loaves and fishes and their passing to the Apostles for distribution. The miracle belongs to those on the north wall of Sant' Apollinare Nuovo, where the monumental Christ of the Early Church, the sun-like God of Roman majesty, works His healings and mysteries. Silhouetted in His purple robe before the golden foil, His head with the inscrutable gaze enhanced by the great halo, He has spread His arms and hands in blessing upon the bread and fish which the Apostles hold. Strength and power flow from the Redeemer to the disciples, assisting in the sacramental act.

Though the Christ is no larger in size than the disciples, His dark shape, in the austerity of the vertical lines which circumscribe His Roman toga, dominates the picture-space and forms a static centre around which the Apostles are grouped in rhythmical symmetry. As they incline their heads towards one another, isolating the figure of Christ, they are at the same time detached and gathered up by the unifying gesture of their Master. Though the frontality of the mosaic and its hieratic spirit exclude the rendering of the communion between Christ and the Apostles, the inward movement of two of the figures is like the closing of the ring.

PLATE 18
BARTOLOMÉ
MURILLO

Not before the Counter Reformation in Italy and in Spain was the *Miracle of the Loaves and Fishes* represented again, and never more poignantly than by Bartolomé Murillo. Here Christ and the Twelve Apostles are foregathered before a backdrop of dark, descending hills above the multitude encamped in the wide sunlit plain. The tender spirituality of Christ blessing the bread, symbol of His communion with the people, leaves no doubt about the sacramental character of the miracle, where the bread, as in the Last Supper, is transformed into His body. Equally the fishes are an ancient symbol of Christ, and this miracle had its special appeal to the theologians of the Counter Reformation and their artists. As the Protestants denied the Real Presence, so the Catholics emphasised the mystery of the Eucharist, and the *Miracle of Loaves and Fishes* is here represented as its anticipation.

Murillo's picture with its clear spatial division is a literal translation of the Gospel text. The exaltation of Christ, the pathos of the Apostles, relieved by the lively boy from whom Peter takes the basket of fish, the transition from the Twelve to the expectant multitude beyond through the outstretched arm of the Apostle, the soft accents of shadow and light, the balance of mass restored by the Spanish family group on the right—all these are signs of Murillo's ripest pictorial style in the service of the Catholic Revival.

PLATE 19
GIOVANNI BATTISTA PITTONI

To view Giovanni Battista Pittoni's *tableau vivant* of eighteenth-century grace and spaciousness after the stern hieratic icon at Ravenna, is to contemplate the whole range of Western pictorial art. It shows how the magical power of the Early Christians was dissipated in twelve centuries of picture-making, and how the religious icon, conceived to cast its spell upon the worshipper and to draw him into the heart of the mystery, has been transformed into a theatrical stage setting, where upon a prospect of radiant landscape, in the shade of feathery trees, the actors recline in graceful groups, as in Watteau's *Embarkation for the Isle of Cytherea.* But for the blaze of Christ's halo, the kneeling Apostle to whom He gives the bread, and a disciple here and there taking the loaves to the recumbent crowd, this worldly gathering of gaily attired people, of children, dogs and a nude ancient with his staff, might be a camp or resting-place of wandering gipsies. The artist of the Rococo imagined the *Miracle of the Loaves and Fishes* not as a sacramental act of mystic significance, but as a festive crowd in an open-air picnic, in a Venetian landscape of exhilarating transparency.

# VI. *Christ at the Sea of Galilee*

"*But the ship was now in the midst of the Sea, tossed with waves: for the wind was contrary. And in the fourth watch of the night, Jesus went unto them, walking on the Sea. And when the Disciples saw him walking on the Sea, they were troubled, saying, It is a spirit: and they cried out for fear. But straightway Jesus spake unto them, saying, Be of good cheer: it is I, be not afraid. And Peter answered him, and said, Lord, if it be thou, bid me come unto thee on the water. And he said, Come. And when Peter was come down out of the ship, he walked on the water, to go to Jesus. But when he saw the wind boisterous, he was afraid: and beginning to sink, he cried, saying, Lord save me. And immediately Jesus stretched forth his hand, and caught him, and said unto him, O thou of little faith, wherefore didst thou doubt?*" (Matthew xiv, 24–31)

PLATE 20
KONRAD WITZ

Our three renderings of the scene present the successive stages of the miracle. Tintoretto describes the stormy Sea of Tiberias and Peter coming down from the boat. The Suebian master, Konrad Witz, shows Peter in the water and Christ rising up before him. Hans von Kulmbach paints the faltering Apostle rescued by the hand of Christ. The earliest of the three is also the most potent. Konrad Witz painted his picture in 1444, his ripest and most suggestive work, enhanced by the contrast between the realistic landscape, a recognisable section on the banks of Lake Geneva, and the ghostly and preternatural shape of Christ. No other painter conveys the suddenness of the apparition and its magic power which terrified the Apostles who "were sore amazed in themselves beyond measure and wondered". This effect is gained by the mere outline of Christ's commanding figure, the grand sweep of his robe, silhouetted against the rippling transparency of the water and topped by the distant peak of the mountain.

This imposing phantom, rising vertically on the near side of the lake, dwarfs the apostolic figures in the boat, the fussy oarsmen and unconcerned fishers, while only Peter seems aware of the apparition, first in the boat and then in the water, where he strains with troubled face to reach the Master. Figures, air and landscape in the painterly style of this great Primitive, melt into one, by means of the reflected lights and shadows cast upon the water, the diminishing lines of trees and the sensitive grading of colours. The imperious shape of Christ, master over men and elements, towers above and merges into the surrounding countryside.

PLATE 21
HANS VON KULMBACH

The formal severity of the Quattrocento has become softened and humanised in the cycle from the life of Peter which Hans von Kulmbach, a follower of Dürer, painted at the beginning of the sixteenth century. His Christ, taking a troubled Peter by the hand and reproving him for his failing faith, lacks the grandeur and the remoteness of Konrad Witz. He is more like a poor school-teacher rescuing a despairing soul from perdition. Christ and His disciples in the boat are marked by the German emphasis on facial expression and feeling, the excessive emotion and piety of mien and gesture, which are the northern substitute for rendering pure existence. How far removed are these troubled and hapless souls with their humid eyes, their turgid locks and knitted brows from the marmoreal strength of Giotto or Piero della Francesca! Yet what a fine painter of landscape is this Hans von Kulmbach, and what a refined colourist. His scene is laid by a mountain lake in the Bavarian Alps, whose peaks echo the rise and fall of the figures, an enchanting symphony of graded blues, in the mysterious haze of sunlit distances, which lend to the scene a poetic quality, as in Altdorfer's painted idylls of legend and history.

PLATE 22
TINTORETTO

In Tintoretto's picture the storm-tossed sky and Sea of Tiberias, the great southern bay and littoral, bounded by cubic rocks and ranges, the inky pitch and glaring crests of the waves, are the real subject. The boat, loaded with small figures, has the expressive shorthand of Byzantine miniatures, and the lofty figure of Christ seems rather to command the storm than to beckon Peter. His slender, elongated shape, boldly and summarily modelled in the light, and balanced by the swaying tree stems on the other bank, is yet the cornerstone of the composition. But more than in the lassitude and assurance of Christ's form and gesture, the magic of the ghostly nocturne lies in the lightning flashes and cloud-fantasies of the storm-ridden sky, the rocking holocaust of the phosphorescent sea.

# VII. *The Healing of the Man born Blind*

"*And as Jesus passed by, he saw a man which was blind from his birth. And his disciples asked him, saying, Master, who did sin, this man, or his parents, that he was born blind? Jesus answered, Neither hath this man sinned, nor his parents: but that the works of God should be made manifest in him. I must work the works of him that sent me, while it is day: the night cometh when no man can work. As long as I am in the world, I am the light of the world. When he had thus spoken, he spat on the ground, and made clay of the spittle, and he anointed the eyes of the blind man with the clay, And said unto him, Go wash in the pool of Siloam* (*which is by interpretation, Sent.*) *He went his way therefore, and washed, and came seeing.*" (John ix, 1–7)

PLATE 23
MOSAIC,
SIXTH CENTURY,
RAVENNA

As the youthful thaumaturgist of the Ravenna mosaics touches with healing hand the eyes of the man born blind, lightly inclining towards him, the latter bends his head and shoulder towards the Redeemer. He, too, wears a purple garment as a sign that henceforth he belongs to Christ. His blind companion repeats the symbolic gesture and strengthens the impact of the group. With sparing means the mosaicist has suggested the groping eagerness of the blind man leaning on his stick and the majestic certainty of Christ's action. Like the leader of the chorus in Greek drama, the witness behind Christ expresses awe and wonder by his movement of head and hand. These four figures in their monumental calm and restraint, though their bodies hardly exist under the voluminous folds of toga and tunic, enact the miracle with such immutable strength, that no later rendering of the scene can rival its rudimentary force and purity of form.

PLATE 24
DUCCIO DI
BUONINSEGNA

Duccio follows another Byzantine scheme, where Christ is accompanied by the Apostles and the blind man appears twice, first in the miracle and then washing his eyes in the pool. The scene is laid in a street of Siena with its grey and pink houses, whose geometrical facets are defined by planes of shadow and light. This gay abstraction of a town with its cubic variety of architectural form, its lit-up walls and dark recesses, its Romanesque archways and Gothic windows, almost dwarfs the solid body of men behind Christ, the antique chorus of Apostles, who stand in their fixity of expression and mask, witnessing the miracle.

Peter and Andrew with their thickset faces and well-groomed beards, the highlights upon their foreheads and cheekbones, are fashioned after a Byzantine formula. In Duccio's *Biblia Pauperum* the Christ is always distinguished by His dark hair and beard and by the formal elegance of His robes, deep rose and ultramarine. The gestures, like those of the blind man who stands on his toes and distorts his hand to show his palm, and by the well gazes up in gratitude for his recovered sight, illustrate, almost paraphrase, the miracle. They speak, to the simple-minded, in unmistakable tones and traditional phrases, even to the lilt and rhythm of formal relationship and spacing.

PLATE 25
EL GRECO

An early work of El Greco's Italian period, painted under the impact of Tintoretto's Venetian *colorito* and vast architectural perspectives, enacts the scene upon a raised and narrow platform. Here a mild and compassionate Christ restores the sight of a blind youth, half-nude and kneeling before Him with such an abandon of trust and of faith, that the healing power seems to flow not only from the hand that anoints the eye, but more so from the arm that will raise the beggar to his feet. To the left, the same youth, a fine Venetian anatomy, is restored to the full vigour of life. He faces his interrogators, some sceptical, some amazed, with his significant gesture heavenwards, in a strong twist of his body, to which a nude man dramatically responds. The commotion of the Apostles opposite is most concentrated in Peter's ecstatic movement of head and hands and, to a lesser degree, in the backview of the man talking over his shoulder. Here the emotional emphasis of the Baroque wells up in the agitation of limbs and expressive faces, it can be felt in the depth of the spatial recession which opens up between the principal groups, breaking down all solid barriers and decentralising the main action, where limbs are pointing outwards and inwards and the eye ranges freely over infinite spaces.

# VIII. *The Delivery of the Keys and Christ's Charge to Peter*

"*When Jesus came into the coasts of Cæsarea Philippi, he asked his disciples, saying, Whom do men say, that I, the Son of man, am? And they said, Some say that thou art John the Baptist, some Elias, and others Jeremias, or one of the Prophets. He saith unto them, But whom say ye that I am? And Simon Peter answered, and said, Thou art the Christ the Son of the living God. And Jesus answered, and said unto him, Blessed art thou Simon Bar-jona: for flesh and blood hath not revealed it unto thee, but my Father which is in heaven. And I say also unto thee, that thou art Peter, and upon this rock I will build my Church: and the gates of hell shall not prevail against it. And I will give unto thee the keys of the kingdom of heaven: and whatsoever thou shalt bind on earth, shall be bound in heaven: whatsoever thou shalt loose on earth, shall be loosed in heaven.*" (Matthew xvi, 13–19)

The Delivery of the Keys to Peter has been presented in Christian art since the Trecento and reached its apogee in Raphael's famous cartoon for the Sistine Tapestry. In 1369 the Veneto-Byzantine Lorenzo Veneziano, follower of Maestro Paolo, the founder of the Venetian School, painted the scene in an altarpiece where Christ is enthroned with Apostles and Angels.

PLATE 26 LORENZO VENEZIANO

Lorenzo's Christ, in His damask mantle of luminous blue with gold ornaments over a roseate robe, is surrounded by much smaller figures of the Twelve Apostles. Only Peter is seen in full length, in a golden mantle at the foot of the throne, receiving the Keys of Heaven. Christ holds in His hand an open book with the words: Tibi dabo claves Regni Coelorum. The Apostles have small contracted heads clinging to their haloes, and the rigid Byzantine gaze from almond-shaped eyes with white dots to mark the iris. There is no space for the Apostles to move, small modelling and individualisation. The beauty of the panel resides in its Eastern ornateness, the sumptuous filigree of design and the fine gradations of colour. The Venetian colour-sensibility appears here for the first time, a fusion of tones and a courtly splendour in the fall of robes. The Byzantine stylisation of form and of type is transformed by a Gothic loveliness of raiment.

To come from the two-dimensional ornateness of the Veneto-Byzantine artist to the "buoyant spaciousness" and heroic figure composition of Perugino's early masterpiece in the Vatican, is like stepping from the prison house into the open air and sunlit radiance. What has happened between 1369 and 1481 is more than a merely aesthetic revolution, a technical advance from the flat, airless and spaceless symbolism of the Trecento to the liberated movement and sculptural existence of grand figures living on the infinite and beauteous surface of the earth. It is a revolution in seeing and perceiving, a freeing of the spirit from medieval fetters, a novel pride in the faculties of man, a discovery of the world around and a scientific conquest of space and perspective. These and kindred achievements of the Renaissance took their measure from the world of Antiquity, and all this is already visible in Perugino's picture.

PLATE 27 PIETRO PERUGINO

Here the Apostles are no more the constrained silhouettes clinging to a background of gold, but yearning youths and Socratic old men in antique drapery, moving freely in the air and the light of an Umbrian summer, before the vastness of sunlit spaces, the rising perspective of the great square which leads the eye to the domed temple. For this great phalanx of men who accompany with muted eloquence Christ's Delivery of the Keys to Peter, are like "architectonic members in the space", subsumed to the noble proportions of the antique structure beyond. Christ's words to Peter, "Super hanc petram aedificabo meam ecclesiam", have become a living reality. In the central axis of the composition, where the first of the Apostles receives the symbol of the keys, that great Church rises up, a soaring pantheon of noble strength. And even though in Perugino's fresco the Apostles stand in studied poses and measured groups, though the pious beauty of youth is a little emphatic and the devoted elders recall Signorelli's types, in spaciousness and proportion and in the new freedom of movement it is an Academy of Renaissance art.

PLATE 28
RAPHAEL

In Raphael's cartoon Peter clasps the Keys of Heaven, but the Christ is the Resurrected, appearing to the disciples and charging Peter with his ministry: "Feed my Sheep." He stands in the full radiant light, a stark and virile apparition, and with forceful gesture gives His command to Peter, while with the other arm He points to a flock of sheep. His eye is fixed on the kneeling Apostle who, a sweeping and fervent shape, gazes upwards at his Master. The grandly conceived throng of Apostles reflects the varying degrees of their belief and acceptance. With full power of individualisation Raphael mirrors awe, love and piety in the foremost group. Then the magical waves issuing from Christ's presence meet with resistance in the doubting Apostle with the dark hair and beard, looking over his shoulder at his companion, who stands motionless and unmoved in hostile rigidity. Then the last lappings of the waves in the sceptical old men who watch the apparition from afar.

Wölfflin in a brilliant chapter of his *Classic Art* wrote how Raphael's "power of psychological expression was quite outside the range of earlier generations". The art of the Early Renaissance knows only one rendering of the apostolic circle around their Master, where the individuality of feature is comparable to Raphael's protagonists: Masaccio's *Tribute Money* in the Carmine Church at Florence. But the rock-like solidity and distinctive character of Masaccio's men is not softened by the expression of soul and of sentiment, which lends to Raphael's figures humanity and ardour, a vibration of the spirit and a literary interpretation of motive which he translates into movement and facial expression. Today psychological inference is no longer appreciated as a vital element in the visual arts, and the grand and "ineloquent" forms of Masaccio have worked a stronger spell than Raphael's emotive gestures and lyrical poses.

PLATE 29
PETER
PAUL
RUBENS

Rubens in the next century painted a number of Christological scenes, always with the same half-draped Christ occupying nearly half of the picture-space, as in the *Four Great Penitents* at Munich or in the *Incredulity of Thomas* at Antwerp. Like Raphael he depicts the Delivery of the Keys and the "Pasce Oves Meas" in one, Christ handing the keys to Peter with his foreshortened right hand and lightly touching the sheep with his left. It is not an ignoble Christ in His smooth and manly beauty and seriousness, though without greater depth of spirit or power of feeling. Only one of the Apostles shows surprise at the appearance of the Resurrected by a glint in his eye, a joyful recognition, while the boyish and golden-haired John and the elder Apostle marvel at Peter's glowing humility and recognition. Perugino's and Raphael's array of heroically draped figures in the ambient air and space is here reduced to a sculptured group of five before a neutral background, a concentrated emphasis on physical presence and bodily splendour, no lofty flight of fancy but a Flemish reality, a human devotion rather than an act of sacramental institution.

PLATE 30
GIOVANNI
BATTISTA
PITTONI

Flamboyancy and a festive exuberance of the Rococo replaced the substantial heaviness of the Baroque, and the Delivery of the Keys becomes in the hands of Giovanni Battista Pittoni a joyful occasion. Heaven and earth, the apostolic band and the angelic host are joined together in a jubilant symphony and the solemnity of the act is transformed into a celestial ballet. The stage where Pittoni's Christ transmits the celestial keys to Peter, accompanied by the pictorial music, the exultant gestures of the Apostles, is essentially the same as the radiant cloudland where triumphant angels and joyful Cupids frolic, and the whole canvas with its toss and tumble, its upward movement, its pointing hands and spreading wings is a hymn of praise. To express this light-hearted and optimistic religion the Rococo artists were gloriously equipped with a command over light and atmosphere, over composite colour and ecstatic movement and Pittoni's work is a pictorial vision of Mozartian cadence, transparency and passion.

# IX. *The Transfiguration*

"*And after six days, Jesus taketh with him Peter, and James, and John, and leadeth them up into an high mountain apart by themselves: and he was transfigured before them. And his raiment became shining, exceeding white as snow: so as no Fuller on earth can white them. And there appeared unto them Elias with Moses: and they were talking with Jesus. And Peter answered, and said to Jesus, Master, it is good for us to be here, and let us make three tabernacles; one for thee, and one for Moses, and one for Elias. For he wist not what to say, for they were sore afraid. And there was a cloud that overshadowed them: and a voice came out of the cloud, saying, This is my beloved Son: hear him. And suddenly when they had looked round about, they saw no man any more, save Jesus only with themselves.*" (Mark ix, 2–8)

PLATE 31 DUCCIO DI BUONINSEGNA

Duccio's Peter and James are like memories of the Palermo mosaic. But they have a far greater figurative presence and expressive force, conveying exultation in Peter, amazement and awe in James. Against the gold ground of an ideal heaven and standing upon the rose-coloured rock, Duccio's Christ in His gold-streaked raiment, His inscrutable gaze, His dark auburn hair and beard is a Byzantine shape. The Sienese painter of the Trecento excels in graceful linear rhythms and luminous colour, the chiselled arabesque of haloes, the flowing contours of robes. Beauty and solemnity of the grave old prophets who pay homage to Christ are poignantly expressed, though their Gothic bodies have no weight and their feet do not cling to the ground.

PLATE 32 FRA ANGELICO DA FIESOLE

The great Florentine artist who painted the *Transfiguration* upon the walls of a cell in the Convent of San Marco at Florence is a traditionalist. Fra Angelico da Fiesole, nearly one hundred and fifty years after Duccio, still avails himself of gold ground and mandorla, and his Apostles beneath the rocky pedestal, where Christ stands in glory, kneel in the symbolic poses of an earlier iconology. They express bewilderment and awe, they shelter from Christ's radiance, they are broadly conceived, with sweeping folds; but their expressive power of individualisation or plastic force has not appreciably advanced. In Angelico's fresco it is the Christ, transfixed as on the Cross, yet spreading His arms in a cosmic embrace, whose immutable grandeur in the mandorla of light surpasses all earlier concepts of the Redeemer, an overwhelming form in the puritanic simplicity of His raiment, unadorned but for the weighty fall of His robes. Angelico, as was his wont, has endowed the Christ with true divinity, a more than human beauty of countenance, a Grecian regularity of feature, a noble fall of hair and beard, the transcending momentum of His gaze. In the visual language of the Quattrocento Angelico's Christ is the real Godhead, by whose side the prophets with whom He holds converse, sculptured heads of marked spirituality, are pure symbols without body.

PLATE 33 GIOVANNI BELLINI

By the side of the transcending majesty of Angelico's Christ, the early Bellini of the Correr Museum, with something of Mantegna's arid plasticity still fresh upon him, impresses more by the mood than the exquisiteness of the composition. Angelico arrived at the imposing grandeur of his figure of Christ by isolating it from the supporting prophets. Bellini's Christ is not only a less noble form, He is closely surrounded by the prophets upon the narrow plateau; and though his elongated form is larger and more radiant than theirs, He has the Roman impassivity of the Paduan School and the marmoreal convolutions of folds. His hand raised in blessing has something claw-like, like Tura's. The prophets by His side gaze up or down in exaltation, as if they too heard the voice from heaven.

Close to the Mantegnesque escarpment the Apostles seem to awake from heavy torpor: Peter in the traditional pose, sheltering his eye from the light, James relaxed and recumbent, John, stretching at the foot of the hill, groping, dazed. His is the most rapturous figure, entranced as in a dream, his silky curls like those of the other John in the Brera Pietà. From this strange beauteous figure the poetry flows over into the Venetian landscape, the sombre, olive plain with the winding road and river under the sunset-sky whose grey pallor melts into greenish blue. It is by the luminous colour and atmosphere, the pristine beauty of the countryside with its leafy plants and single trees that the harshness of rock and figures is dissolved into a mood of solemnity and stillness.

In the Naples *Transfiguration*, painted about twenty years later, Bellini attained to the fullness of his own mature style. His transfigured Christ is no longer raised upon a barren mound, but stands elated like an antique Orante upon the bountiful earth, before a vast prospect of meadow, hills and sky. He is no less exalted for being part of the creation, no less remote for being close to the fruitful earth and to the dwellings of labouring man and beast. Only Bellini's Christ is the Son of Man as of God, in communion with both, but none the less solitary and apart. The prophets by His side stand in noble lassitude and humility, the Apostles hear but do not see. PLATE 34 GIOVANNI BELLINI

This breadth of painterly vision, this fusion of the human figure with the inhabited earth and the wide horizons, in composite tones of glowing colour, which is the glory of the Venetian School, was also Perugino's secret by which he ennobled his often conventional figures. But the *Transfiguration*, which he painted late in life for the Collegio del Cambio at Perugia, lacks the aid of his silvery distances, the slate-blue hills and fine-leafed trees of his native Umbria. In the Cambio there is no landscape, except for the barren mound and the cloud-streaked sky; all the emphasis is on the figures, their solid shapes, their classical symmetry, their yearning, their traditional poses. The lofty Christ in a mandorla of golden rays, lightly stepping upon a bank of clouds, is the meek and resigned Redeemer of pietistic religion, a graceful and delicate form between the sturdy prophets by his side. PLATE 35 PIETRO PERUGINO

Among the Apostles Peter and James are attitudinising conventions. But John in his pale lilac tunic and moss-green robe, his smooth auburn hair and firmly modelled head, is almost free from the Peruginesque sentiment. He is a novel invention in Perugino's repertoire of saintly figures. His body has real existence and rounded form, his slight and noble face reflects the vision from above; his golden locks are foiled by his strong columnar neck. Gazing upwards, he shelters his eye from the light which fills the sky above the darkened hill. As the Apostles are separated from their transfigured Lord by their earthly existence and by the immensity of heaven, so they are again conjoined to the Christ by the gentleness and compassion which emanate from His figure.

Perugino's compositional scheme followed an archaic pattern, his creative imagination was limited, and his Christ, though His garment flutters in the breeze and His hands are raised in invocation, stands transfixed within the Byzantine mandorla of light. It was left to Raphael, his one-time pupil, to bequeath, as the last work of his genius, the most inspired solution of the subject. Vasari saw in Raphael's Christ, soaring to heaven in a blaze of light, the divine essence of the Three Persons of the Trinity. The Redeemer no longer holds converse with the prophets upon the mountain within sight of His nearest disciples. His arms spread out in a wide embrace of yearning and fulfilment, He has left the earth and rises towards the Father whom His exalted gaze already perceives. Only Raphael among all painters of the Christian era conveys the communion of the transfigured Christ with the Father, His mystical elevation, where the eye, no longer turned towards His earthly followers, reflects the vision of the empyrean. The prophets of the Old Testament circle like planets around their sun, seized by the same whirl of movement, reflecting the same radiance. Only the Apostles, cowering below on the darkened hill, are unable to bear the light. They must cling to the ground and protect their vision in utter bewilderment and despair, that the Master has left the earth. Thus is the circle accomplished, a wheel of light, a centripetal movement around the Godhead who, with flaming hair, the ecstatic certainty of His eye, with arms receiving and received, hails-in the coming of a new aeon. PLATE 36 RAPHAEL

# X. The Tribute Money

"*And when they were come to Capernaum, they that received tribute money, came to Peter, and said, Doth not your master pay tribute? He saith, Yes. And when he was come into the house, Jesus prevented him, saying, What thinkest thou, Simon? of whom do the kings of the earth take custom or tribute? of their own children, or of strangers? Peter saith unto him, Of strangers. Jesus saith unto him, Then are the children free. Notwithstanding, lest we should offend them, go thou to the Sea, and cast an hook, and take up the fish that first cometh up; and when thou hast opened his mouth, thou shalt find a piece of money: that take, and give unto them for me, and thee.*" (Matthew xvii, 24–7)

PLATE 37
MASACCIO

This scene has inspired what is perhaps the greatest single advance in Renaissance painting: Masaccio's fresco in the Cappella Brancacci at the Carmine Church in Florence. The moment is represented when Christ commands Peter to pay the required tax to the Roman soldier at the gates of Capernaum. With imperious gesture He tells Peter to go to the Lake of Gennesaret to extract the coin from the mouth of the fish, while the Apostle, looking at the Master with sustained passion, repeats His gesture. There are two subsidiary scenes. On the left Peter kneels down by the lakeside, opening the fish's jaw, his head bent over the task, while on the right he scornfully pays his coin to the jeering soldier.

But the heart of the deepest tension is the great circle of men around Christ, each of them wrapped in a wide mantle, which gives them their solid Roman appearance and dignity. They are stark individual characters, determined men of action with wills of their own, bearded ancients or splendid youths, united around their Master by the strength of their dedication. Moreover, they are the first sculptural shapes of the Florentine School, broadly chiselled in the round out of hard, rock-like matter, their square and rugged heads fashioned by the light and moulded by shadow; and though they are portraits of Renaissance men, an unyielding race, varied in mood and in physical form, they stand like human pillars of the invisible Church around them. Men such as these seem to create the space in which they move, the reddish earth on which they stand with such proud possession, the hills descending to the lake and punctuated by trees, the snow-capped mountains beyond. In this harsh and barren setting Masaccio saw the first Christians move, a primeval race of men, locked in a close circle of followers around their Head, a brotherhood forged for conquest.

This pictorial realisation of the Christian story was possible for Masaccio through his command over space, mass, movement and character. He and not Giotto was the first to paint "al naturale", not to imitate things as they are, as Vasari wrote, but to give to the human figure a heightened reality greater than life. This new realism which gave to figures that wide range of personal expression and gesture, also extended to the supernatural, and Masaccio's Christ is not a stylish idealisation but a leader of men with marked individual features.

# XI. *Christ and the Apostles Entering Jerusalem*

"*And the Disciples went, and did as Jesus commanded them, And brought the Ass, and the colt, and put on them their clothes, and they set him thereon. And a very great multitude spread their garments in the way, others cut down branches from the trees, and strawed them in the way. And the multitudes that went before, and that followed, cried, saying, Hosanna to the son of David: Blessed is he that cometh in the Name of the Lord; Hosanna in the highest.*" (Matthew xxi, 6–9)

PLATE 38 MOSAIC, TWELFTH CENTURY, PALERMO

Christ's Entry into Jerusalem forms the climax of the Christological festival cycle of mosaic art in Italy and in Greece. Christ riding on a colt blesses the multitudes who receive Him at the Gates of Jerusalem, while children spread their garments and lay palm branches at the foot of the procession. It is the courtly taste of the Norman kings in Sicily which dictates the style of the mosaics in the Royal Palace at Palermo. Christ on His mount rides into the city like an Eastern potentate, proudly and ceremoniously led by his chancellor and followed by the cortège of his ministers. This courtly train proceeds on golden carpets strewn with twigs of palm leaf and, beneath it, four lively boys with short cropped hair and Oriental round heads bustle to lay branches and garments on the path of the king, while one of them, in the exuberance of the feast, strips himself of his coat.

Christ and the Apostles move in line with the descending hill, and the realistic detail, like the romping children, the ass straining its long neck and the feathery palm tree, make a decorative pattern as in tapestry, where every nook is filled with leaf and flower. In the twelfth-century mosaic of the Palatina the severity of Byzantine icons is allayed by the festive solemnity of the procession, its restrained splendour and gaiety, moving in the narrow space between the hill and the marbled city, where the triumphant Saviour and His companions are welcomed by the Hierosolomite Elders and a woman at the gate.

The Entry into Jerusalem became the favourite subject of the Sienese School. Duccio, Barna da Siena and Pietro Lorenzetti have all indulged their native sense for gorgeous display, for festive crowds and glittering buildings, translating the sober language of the Byzantine mosaics into the gaudy costumes, the Trecento architecture and the holiday mood of contemporary Siena. Duccio's rendering remained unsurpassed. He has borrowed the Byzantine scheme, but transformed it into a Sienese reality. His Christ, with the throng of Apostles following close on His heels, rides uphill into the city along the wall through the open gate, where the excited crowd welcomes the Lord. From the small empty garden beneath, to the domed cathedral, there is one syncopated upward surge, with boys spreading garments and waving olive branches, others looking across the walls, out of windows and down from trees. Whether we look through the embattled arch to the pink houses and turrets of Siena or upon the knitted brows of old men, the white turbans, the scarlet and blue tunics, the boys hanging in the trees like ripe fruit, or the serried advance of Christ with the anxious Apostles—it is the popular agitation of a great civic event that Duccio portrays, a delirious crowd welcoming their king to the golden city by the pearly gate.

PLATE 39 DUCCIO DI BUONINSEGNA

After Duccio's tumult and exuberance of small figures—Giotto's selective tranquillity and *grandiosità*. The Byzantine echoes grow fainter, though the pattern remains unchanged. Where Duccio illustrated with multitudinous detail, Giotto creates by strength of relief the salient features of the story: a masterful

PLATE 40 GIOTTO DI BONDONE

Christ, a spiritual king, blessing the people who pay homage at the gate. To convey the vital moment, the religious solemnity, Giotto needed no crowds, no details of genre; only the beauty and majesty of the Saviour, the functional line and sweep of His arm raised in blessing, the upright nobility of His gait, the weight of His body astride the colt, and close to Him a small group of Apostles, full-length figures, massive, powerful in their gravity of mien, their regularity of feature, their fixed Byzantine gaze and the generous amplitude of their robes. The measured austerity of this group is balanced by the few representative citizens opposite, who hail the coming of Christ. Men and women bow their heads in veneration, children take off their cloaks or greet the Saviour with olive branches. Each figure is marked by solidity of structure and functional gesture, by mass and volume which, even without scientific perspective, create the space between the foreground and the city gate. There are no hills, no landscape background, but the two single trees, where boys cut branches, suggest a measure of depth and recession. But above all it is Giotto's rarefied grouping, his selective design and broadly modelled figures, which endow his story with processional dignity and "sacramental intentness".

# XII. *Christ Washing the Feet of the Apostles*

*"He riseth from supper, and laid aside his garments, and took a towel, and girded himself. After that, he poureth water into a bason, and began to wash the disciples' feet, and to wipe them with the towel wherewith he was girded. Then cometh he to Simon Peter: and Peter saith unto him, Lord, dost thou wash my feet? Jesus answered, and said unto him, What I do, thou knowest not now: but thou shalt know hereafter. Peter saith unto him, Thou shalt never wash my feet. Jesus answered him, If I wash thee not, thou hast no part with me. Simon Peter saith unto him, Lord, not my feet only, but also my hands and my head."* (John xiii, 4–9)

The medieval mosaic showing Christ washing the feet of the Apostles in the Cathedral of Monreale is the prototype of mid-Byzantine iconography which Duccio followed closely in his Sienese altarpiece. Otto Demus saw in the Palermo mosaics the transformation of the neo-Hellenistic ideal into an "agitated Baroque", whose hallmark is the restless linearism of folds and the emphatic modelling of cheeks, hips and knees, "an inorganic revolt of individual parts".

PLATE 41 MOSAIC, TWELFTH CENTURY, PALERMO

The Washing of the Feet is only related in the Fourth Gospel, and the moment is represented when Peter exclaims: "Lord, not my feet only, but also my hands and my head." It is, like the Last Supper, a sacramental act of communion between Christ and the disciples, without which they have no part with Him. Thus Peter's hand is raised to his head in the expressive realism of gesture which proclaims his zeal. Christ dries his feet with a towel in a dignified forward slant of His body. Three Apostles are seated upon a lofty bench, while others, varying in character and in age, are standing behind, foiled by the geometrical divisions of the architecture. From the left two Apostles approach with a jug of water, completing the rhythmical pattern of the figure composition. These two upright figures with their classicist stance will reappear in Giotto's fresco, but they are absent from Duccio's painting.

PLATE 42 DUCCIO DI BUONINSEGNA

By lowering the Apostles' bench before which Christ is kneeling and by grouping all the disciples together on one side of the panelled room, Duccio has heightened the dramatic intensity of the scene. The three foremost disciples are similarly poised as in Palermo, but the expressionism of all faces, the wonderment in the eyes, the eager bend of heads, the perplexity of hands are immeasurably increased. These humble disciples hardly believe their eyes, and Peter clasping his head, clings to the bench with a rigid distortion of his left arm and hand. The urgency of Christ, exhorting Peter, corresponds to the bewilderment of the Apostle. Thus the mosaic prototype has been transformed by a great dramatic artist into a human document, the ceremonious figures of Monreale are made to express quite human emotions, impetuous loyalty in Peter, as the meaning of the new sacrament and the pending betrayal grips their slow-working minds.

PLATE 43 GIOTTO DI BONDONE

Drama, psychology are not Giotto's means of rendering the Washing of the Apostles' Feet in the Scrovegni Chapel at Padua. The huddled group of Apostles, their wrinkled faces, their worried expression, the whole Gothic-Byzantine inheritance of Duccio is swept aside by the Roman sense for mass and solidity of figures, for breadth of form and sacramental dignity which Giotto had imbibed in the School of Cimabue and Cavallini. Here the Christ kneels in the centre, clasping the leg of Peter, whom He regards with persuasive force, with commanding power. Peter, a fully rounded shape, moulded by the structural folds of his ample cloak, is a rock-like figure, firm as granite and rooted to the chair, unlike Duccio's Apostle with his upward movement of leg and arm, who seems to be lifted from his bench. He too gazes at the Christ in dawning comprehension; for Giotto has rendered the moment following upon Peter's protest, "Lord, Thou shalt never wash my feet."

The other Apostles are grouped around the room in mute and solemn circle, and the grandest of them opposite Peter, who bends low to loosen his sandal, is a monumental shape of powerful sculptural mass, such as will not be seen in Italian painting before Michelangelo's Patriarchs. The two youthful Apostles carrying water, as in the Monreale mosaic, are now drawn into the circle, placidly upright like statues, conveying no emotion as the rest of them. Therein lies the fundamental difference between Giotto and Duccio, who worked at the same time and only at a short distance from one another, that Giotto's cubic and space-creating shapes, in their heightened reality, their Romanesque strength of relief, convey a greater sense of being, of sheer existence than Duccio's expressive actors in the Play of Christ's Passion. These are two vital forms of image-making, monumental the one and intimately human the other, even to the details of genre, like the sandals on the floor and the towel hanging from a rail.

Other presentations of the subject during the course of the Quattrocento, like Vecchietta's, dehumanise the figures, while surrounding them with a glittering Sienese elegance of ornamental effects. The large, sober forms of Giotto are forgotten and the Apostles, in monotonous lifelessness, are strung around the walls of a room whose blue and starry ceiling and gold decorum are the chief attraction.

PLATE 44 GIOVANNI AGOSTINO DA LODI

Not before the coming of the Renaissance to northern Italy can we trace a new concept of the scene, when Giovanni Agostino da Lodi, a pupil of Bramantino, in the year 1500 painted his classical composition of grand figures of marked character and individuality. But though the washing of the Apostle's feet takes place in the symmetrical centre, though the youthful Christ is a manly figure, and Peter, clad in a golden mantle, protests his unworthiness with restrained eloquence, the real subjects are the Apostles, standing behind in a double row, who seem to hail from one of Leonardo's sketch-books. Here the bearded patriarch with his book, in a glowing red mantle, high priest or magician, is the dominant figure. As he looks down with eyes half-closed and serried lips, his domed brow reflecting the light, his face modelled in soft chiaroscuro, ageless and inscrutable, he is not aware of the youth by his side in a pale green mantle, who gazes upon the scene, while half-listening to the words of the tempter behind.

The caricature of evil by which the painter has singled out Judas, like other characters among the apostolic band, is a free fantasy upon Leonardo's portrayal of human passion. Like Signorelli in the *Last Judgment* at Orvieto Cathedral, the painter has represented the tempter whispering into the ear of an innocent youth, whom another Apostle touches lightly, as if to draw him back into the circle, where Christ admits the disciples into the mystery of His own Life and Passion. The Apostles are grand virile shapes, philosophers of the market place, not humble fishermen; some are protesting their faith, others stare icily into space; some are suspicious and hostile, others eager and loving, like the youth with the silky locks who holds the towel; some noble and statuesque—Renaissance individuals all with a searching mind, a will of their own, pondering, judging, ready to follow or to make the great refusal. This rather inflexible design records in powerful human shapes a changing scale of religious certainty.

PLATE 45 TINTORETTO

After the classic formula of Giovanni Agostino da Lodi, more rigidly classic perhaps because he was an eclectic, a youthful work of Tintoretto illustrates the compositional decentralisation of the Baroque. The principal episode has moved off-centre, balanced by a secondary incident on the left, Apostles are scattered in groups of two about the room, to indicate depth and recession, and the scene assumes a leisurely, almost casual character. That is the nature of the Baroque: a dissolution of the classical order and symmetry, an unleashing of forces moving in and out of the picture, a preoccupation with space, a yearning for the Infinite which breaks down walls and barriers and frees the central vista, pushing the main actors to the side. Tintoretto treats the figure of Christ with this new emphasis on an outward and diagonal movement which leaves the centre free. Peter approaching from the extreme right is precariously poised as he places one foot into the basin. Opposite, two further Apostles repeat the action according to Christ's word: "If I then your Lord and Master have washed your feet, ye also ought to wash one another's feet." But the centre, raised into prominence by the light, is formed by two aged Apostles reading at the table, while to the left and right the dark interior opens, to let in the Venetian sky and distance with other phantom figures and Renaissance buildings.

If one recalls the monotonous double row of Apostles, seated upon a high bench and loosening their sandals, while Christ on the extreme left dries the feet of Peter, in the twelfth-century mosaic at San Marco, Tintoretto's arrangement appears as the final dissolution of the hieratic as well as the classical styles. Duccio and also Giotto had grouped the Apostles in a bunch, as it were, marvelling at and preparing for the Washing of the Feet. Tintoretto, with his interest in spatial relationship and his realistic sense of probability and action, could not bear to present the Apostles as an impassive group of onlookers, but scattered the twelve all over the magnificent marble hall, in coherent groups of twos or fours, reading, meditating, or pulling the socks off one another's feet. Such variety he enhanced by a glorious scale of composite colour accents: the fiery red of Judas, standing solitary against a column in the middle distance, Christ's crimson and blue, Peter's orange and blue, and between them the warm emerald green of the disciple. The growing naturalism of the age favoured a scene of such casual life-likeness, rather than the hieratic rigidity of an earlier iconography.

# XIII. *The Last Supper*

"*And in the evening he cometh with the twelve. And as they sat, and did eat, Jesus said, Verily I say unto you, one of you which eateth with me, shall betray me. And they began to be sorrowful, and to say unto him, one by one, Is it I? And another said, Is it I? And he answered, and said unto them, It is one of the twelve, that dippeth with me in the dish.*
"*And as they did eat, Jesus took bread, and blessed, and brake it, and gave to them, and said, Take, eat: this is my body. And he took the cup, and when he had given thanks, he gave it to them: and they all drank of it. And he said unto them, This is my blood of the new Testament, which is shed for many.*" (Mark xiv, 17–20 and 22–4)

PLATE 46
MOSAIC,
SIXTH CENTURY,
RAVENNA

The mosaic in Sant' Apollinare Nuovo is the oldest, the most archaic representation of the Last Supper. It combines the sacramental offering of Christ's body with the impact of His word upon the Apostles: "One of you which eateth with me, shall betray me." Not the paschal lamb, but bread and two fishes are the mystical meal which Christ shares with His disciples. He is not the youthful, sunlike God of the miracles and the healings, not the round-faced, radiant Olympian, but the bearded Sufferer of the Passion, haggard and grave, the Son of Man. In His purple robe the recumbent Christ, like Judas opposite, is silhouetted against the golden background. Judas alone is seen in profile, as he will remain in Western art up to Leonardo. As the Saviour has raised His hand and spoken the fatal word, Peter responds with significant gesture: "Lord, is it I?" The disciples are closely arrayed, and the four nearest to Christ gaze at Him intently. Then the movement of heads and eyes flows towards Judas and from him back to Christ. In the secret correspondence between the Ravenna mosaics on opposite walls of the nave, the *Last Supper* is the first of the Passion scenes, as the *Marriage at Cana*, which foreshadowed the mystery of the wine, was the first of the miracles.

Formally the pattern of the mosaic, entirely composed of squares and a semicircle, reveals a rare compactness of artistic abstraction. To express drama and mystery the primitive artist had at his disposal only line and colour. He made the serried row of Apostles cling to the arch of the table and suggested spiritual motive only by a change of direction, the slant of bodies, the glint of eyes. As for colour, they are of liturgical purity and splendour: bluish white, dark purple and gold.

The C-shaped table and the wide sweep of the Apostles sitting around it is the Byzantine prototype, which was also adopted by the master of the twelfth-century mosaic in Monreale. Here Judas hurries along at the near side of the table in a stooping posture to receive the sop according to Christ's word: "He that dippeth his hand with me in the dish, the same shall betray me." Western art replaced the semicircular table by a rectangular one, and, in San Marco at Venice, Christ and Peter are sitting at opposite ends, while the Apostles are facing the beholder and the near side of the table is left free.

PLATE 47
DUCCIO DI
BUONINSEGNA
PLATE 48
GIOTTO DI
BONDONE

Duccio as well as Giotto follows the Western tradition, but the Apostles are now occupying the benches on both sides. In Giotto's Scrovegni fresco Christ is at the corner and Judas dips his hand into the same dish. But Duccio places Christ in the centre and Judas opposite, who raises his hand to take the sop from that of Christ, which is stretched out towards him. In all but the Ravenna mosaic John lies asleep at the breast of Christ, according to the Fourth Gospel: "There was leaning on Jesus' bosom one of his disciples whom Jesus loved." Among Giotto's Apostles there is no drama or consternation, but only serenity and calm. Duccio portrays the agitation which Christ's announcement of the coming betrayal causes among the disciples, in a variety of mien and contorted gesture. Their flowing hair and beards, their craned necks and angular movements reflect the intensity of their emotion. In Giotto's fresco placidity and stillness reign, where Peter casts a questioning glance at the Lord and the Apostles look at one another in mute solemnity. Their hands are resting on the table and their powerfully constructed forms, of ample girth and Romanesque solidity, hardly betray the stirring of the soul.

Not many years after, a follower of Pietro Lorenzetti painted the *Last Supper* and other scenes from Christ's Passion on the walls of the Lower Church at San Francesco in Assisi. In the octagonal room amidst the profusion of red and gold under the blue-starred firmament where the Apostles sit in a full circle around the table, an echo of Giotto's plastic volumes can still be felt, though the overweening impression is that of decorum and rhythmical grouping. And here for the first time, besides the architectural dainties of the Sienese artist, some elements of genre are introduced, a serving man and woman in the doorway and a scullion wiping dishes by the blazing fire in the kitchen parlour. Such irrelevant details will be in great favour with artists of the Seicento who, like this early Sienese decorator, allow their domestic pets to intrude upon the most sacred scene.

PLATE 49 Ascribed to PIETRO LORENZETTI

While the later Sienese, like Barna and Sassetta, painted variations on Duccio's theme, it was in the Flemish north that the Last Supper received a poignantly sincere and novel rendering. The Altar of the Holy Sacrament which Dirk Bouts painted for Louvain Cathedral in 1464, is the principal contribution to the subject by a Flemish Primitive in the following of Jan van Eyck and Rogier van der Weyden. In a well-lit and well-appointed Gothic interior the Twelve Apostles are gathered at table in neat and orderly symmetry around the Christ who makes the offering of the Eucharist. It is the Flemish concept of Christ, meek, and soulful-devout, the Lamb of God; and His disciples are of the same pious disposition, humble and submissive. The Redeemer in the central axis of the composition, in stillness of mystical elevation, institutes the symbolic offering. The Apostles, typified in character, mood and bearing, holding their narrow, Gothic bodies rigidly upright, reflect the solemn moment in sanctimonious earnestness. Not a breath of drama or of compassion animates their faces, but only a northern inwardness, a spiritual state. The Apostles nearest to Christ are more emphatically turned towards Him, others are more remote and alone with their thoughts. The vacant space at the near side of the table leaves the view open towards the Christ, the Eucharistic symbols and the panelled Cross behind. Daylight falls from the side windows into the spacious room, and the patterned floor, the Gothic doorway lead into the forecourt without. The assistants, equally serious and devout as the protagonists at the table, are portrait characters, and the man with the tight-fitting cap, standing in the portico, is the painter himself.

PLATE 50 DIRK BOUTS

Bouts conceived the *Last Supper* in a Flemish interior of immaculate design and perspective, with refined details, like the bronze lustre hanging from the beams, the Gothic frieze carved in stone. He painted the Communion of the Apostles, their devoutness and dedication, simple folk without guile, Christ's flock, who will deny and desert Him at Golgotha, but who are here unified by a spiritual bond.

Ten years later, another Fleming, Justus van Ghent, painted the *First Communion of the Apostles* for the Corpus Domini at Urbino and Duke Federigo da Montefeltro. Justus had come to Urbino from the city of Hugo van der Goes, and in his first altarpiece for the Italian patron, he endeavoured to graft southern eloquence and monumentality upon his Flemish inheritance. He departed from the fixed iconography of the Last Supper by placing the communion table in the altar region of a Renaissance church, and made the Apostles kneel before Christ in a sweeping semicircle, instead of sitting rigidly upright at table. Christ, an impressive shape in his simple greyish-blue robe with long tubular folds, strides out towards the Apostles. Contrite and submissive, bearded denizens of the road, they surround the Saviour, bending low, eager to receive the communion. Only John stands by the table, clasping the flask of wine, and near him a dwarfish, worried Judas, averting his face. Two Rogier-like angels in voluminous, wrinkled garments float in the air above, while from the far corner, like a breath of wind, enter Duke Federigo and his counsellors, in red and gold embroidered robes—an incursion of Renaissance pageant into the solemnity of the Last Supper.

PLATE 51 JUSTUS VAN GHENT

Justus van Ghent had mixed freely with Italian and Spanish artists, at work in the Palace of Urbino. But in the *First Communion of the Apostles* there is only a thin Italian varnish, perceptible in the play of hands, the southern vivaciousness of the courtiers, the slender and noble shape of Christ. Elsewhere the northern gloom and primitive stiffness of Bouts prevail, and the concentrated drama of life, which Hugo van der Goes imparted to his unkempt and bewildered Apostles.

PLATE 52 Ascribed to HANS HOLBEIN THE YOUNGER

Shortly after his arrival in Basle from medieval Augsburg (1515) Hans Holbein the Younger painted *Scenes from Christ's Passion*, and the *Last Supper*, which, as a work of the Late Gothic, must find its place here. It illustrates the Teutonic ruthlessness of spirit in which the young Holbein interpreted Scriptures, and also the state of his aesthetic sensibility before it had mellowed in contact with the art of northern Italy. In the stormy congregation of the *Last Supper* Holbein freely uses Flemish and German types, Grünewald's above all, and Hugo van der Goes', and adorns the barren brick of the angular room with Renaissance motifs and pillars.

The gathering of the Apostles with its stark realism, its crudity of mask, its tempestuous drama, is not free from vulgarity, where a grimacing John has slipped under the table, and Judas—a distorted satyr-like Judas, to whom Christ gives the sop—seizes the table as if he wanted to overthrow it. One scholar has seen in the menacing fury of Judas a revolt against the Betrayal, and in the Christ of the Agony "who resembles him like a brother" a protest against martyrdom. Holbein has not shrunk from an exasperated veracity and caricature to express the chaos and disillusion of his own spiritual state, and laid bare the possibilities of the German soul at a moment when all religious imagery was threatened by the iconoclasts from within and without. For in the tragedy that is enacted here Judas is the protagonist, in whom brutishness and the lower passions are joined to such savage force, that the ineffectual piety of his opponents will not avail, though Peter stares at him with knitted brow and clenched fists. The German painter has presented Judas as one fallen from grace and in uproar against his fate, the rebel-angel whose form spells chaos, revenge and the dissolution of the spiritual order.

PLATE 53 ERCOLE DEI ROBERTI

If the religious works of the young Holbein present shapes essentially northern, Ercole dei Roberti was a classical Italian in whom the harshness of Ferrara and the Romanism of Padua combined to create a *Last Supper* of concentrated momentum. He grouped the Apostles on three sides of the table in a room of classical measure, framing the ethereal figure of Christ by a powerful Renaissance arch, supported by pilasters. The Apostles not only fill the architectural space with its noble symmetry and proportion, lit from an invisible window on the left, they are its measure, they seem to create it. The severity of architectural design is matched by the precision of form, the circumscribed individuality of the Twelve in varied attitudes of contemplation or prayer. Only Peter and John, by the quarter-turn of their bodies, are drawn towards the centre, the others by look and gesture—absorbed, pondering, exalted—and by the expressive language of hands, are so many isolated figures in space, conjoined at the table by the mystery of the Eucharist and their searching of heart, after the announcement of the Betrayal. In this psychological gradation of character and spirit, Judas is set apart at the edge of the table, a dark and tortured shape, seeing the nightmare vision of his terrible fate. But though the Apostles are forceful and solitary existences, they are spiritually united, and though they look outwards and inwards, they converge towards the Master, who in a solemn gesture blesses the symbol of their communion.

PLATE 54 ANDREA DEL CASTAGNO

The fifteenth century in Florence created three major representations of the Last Supper. It is as if Castagno's work in Sant' Apollonia of 1457 and Ghirlandaio's in Ognissanti of 1480 were preparations for the climacteric of Leonardo at the end of the century. Florentine science, anatomy and perspective, and the sculptural ideal which Donatello imparted to the painters of his time and of his city, had formed Andrea del Castagno. The fierceness of isolated figures, the nervous tension of line which circumscribes form, the metallic precision and polished surfaces of marble entablature lend to his *Cenacolo* its immaculate and calculated perfection. By constructing an oblong room in deep recession with walls foreshortened and diminishing ceiling, he anticipated Leonardo. At the long horizontal table the

Apostles sit in brooding isolation, heroic shapes, incisively modelled, in antique drapery, pondering the word that has been spoken, enclosed in their own grave countenance. Only the central group of Christ, John and Peter breaks the icy spell, where the Redeemer raises His hand in blessing and gazes upon the sleeping Apostle, a saddened image of *amor fati*. Peter is drawn into the group by the half-turn of his figure and the inquiring glance, but Judas sits alone on the near side of the table, a dark and threatening shape, inexorable destroyer of the kingdom of love.

Ghirlandaio in Ognissanti followed a similar iconographical scheme of Christ and the Apostles sitting back to the wall at an oblong table with Judas isolated before it, but now the ends are projecting into the room and the two great Renaissance arches are letting in the light and the sky with birds and ornamental trees. Christ raises His hand and the announcement has been made, for the Apostles in groups of two are searching their hearts and protesting their loyalty, while Judas looks with a challenge to Peter who appears to attack him. Ghirlandaio was a more facile and superficial artist, and his Apostles have not the weight and the depth of Castagno's characters, nor their grimness and chiselled plasticity. Nor are they gathered up in dramatic groups like Leonardo's Apostles, and their assembly lacks a centre, for Ghirlandaio placed his Christ to the left of the great buttress supporting the vault. Yet by his "calm presentation of simple figures", by pleasant raiment and airy spaciousness, by equal balance and meticulous detail Ghirlandaio's *Last Supper* is a noble composition.

PLATE 55
DOMENICO
GHIRLANDAIO

If the earlier masters left some doubt as to the precise moment portrayed, if Castagno shows each member wrapt in contemplation, Ghirlandaio hardly allows a shadow of the forthcoming doom to darken the Apostles' faces—there can be no doubt that Leonardo concentrates all his power on rendering the emotion which grips the disciples on hearing that a traitor dwells in their midst. The announcement which throws the staid gathering into confusion and causes that vast range of mimic abhorration is made the more efficacious by the contrast of the tumult with Christ's transcending calm. He who has spoken those terrifying words is Himself entirely withdrawn, in the midst of His daily companions, His hands spread upon the table, as if to show the stigmata of His pending Passion.

PLATE 56
LEONARDO
DA VINCI

No flying birds or ornamental shrubs detract from the austerity of the room with its oblique walls and open door at the back, which frames the central figure of Christ in dominant isolation. To effect this, Leonardo did not shrink from severing the favourite disciple from the side of the Master and joins him in a group with Judas. The emphatic movement of the nearest Apostles away from the centre, strongest in the figure of James the Great who throws up his arms and stares upon the invisible nail-wounds in Christ's hands, corresponds to the backward thrust of Judas who rests his athletic arm upon the table, clasping the money-bag in his hand. Peter's contorted shape bends towards John to whisper in his ear, and on the other side the youthful Philip also bends towards the Master, protesting his innocence and affection. Towards the extremities of the table the agitation subsides and at each end a quiet whole-length figure stems the great tidal waves.

The *Cenacolo* must be considered the last universal icon of Occidental Christianity. It casts its spell by concentrating on figures greater than life and on the most powerful embodiment of emotional content. The modern pilgrim to the refectory of the Dominican monks in Santa Maria delle Grazie at Milan may sum up his impressions thus: a tremendous illusion of depth is conveyed by the convergence of walls and ceiling towards the centre. This room is almost as great a revelation as the heroic figures within. Its geometrical astringency like a huge magical box, the planes of light upon the vertical divisions of wall, help to unify the groups of Apostles, and here the vehement language of hands contains all the drama and all the expression of spirit: a picture of violent disquiet, with the noble becalmed Christ as a powerful contrast, immutable and sublime above the earthly strife of man.

The *Communion of the Apostles*, which Luca Signorelli painted in 1512 for the Compagnia del Gesù of his native Cortona, is the final page of the Renaissance in the visualisation of that particular moment of Christ's Passion. It is not a *Last Supper* with its sequence of motives, its divided attention, its exacting iconography. Signorelli in his ripest, most tenderly human and most sustained religious style, has

PLATE 57
LUCA
SIGNORELLI

conceived the First Communion in its sacramental significance: Christ offering the Host to His chosen disciples, and the devoutness and exaltation of the Twelve, as the central mystery of the Christian cult is revealed to them.

Before an opening, formed by the receding arches and ornamental pilasters, the commanding figure of Christ is silhouetted against the Umbrian sky. In classical *contrapposto* He strides towards the Apostles kneeling on his right, who receive the Host with such an emotional ardour that their whole being is merged in the act of worship. As Christ inclines towards them, so they bow their heads in adoration, and their faces glow with saintly beauty. To His left two groups of Apostles accompany the Communion with emphatic glances and gestures, eager to perceive and to comprehend, and here an older disciple initiates a brother into the mystery of the Eucharist, one of Signorelli's most radiant shapes, in the bloom of youth, the rich crown of hair, the look of yearning. By contrast, Judas cringes in the forefront of the picture, haggard, with shifty eyes and bony skull, and a movement of diabolic scurrility, placing the Host into his money-bag.

Thus Signorelli painted the Apostles' Communion as a body of inspired men, arrayed around their Master in loving concord, in devotional fervour; and by his command over movement and space-composition he expressed the life of the spirit in the movement of the body and opposed the calm, heroic and ruling figure of Christ to the ecstatic abandon of the Apostles.

PLATE 58 PAOLO VERONESE

Interior drama and spirituality are not the qualities to be looked for in Veronese, but verve and decorative splendour and that "frank and joyous worldliness" which the Renaissance imparted to religious painting. His *Last Supper* is an assembly of great-limbed agitated men in sumptuous robes, crowding around the table in the open-air portico of an inn, where every nook is filled not only with the protagonists of the story, but also with servants, cellarers, a Negro, a dog, a girl giving alms to a beggar and other irrelevancies. In the narrative oblong frieze Christ is seated at the extremity, giving the sop to Judas who kneels before Him, a burly, savage figure with bared shoulders. In order to free the view to the Apostles on the far side of the table, Veronese made the figures on the near side prostrate themselves in an almost Oriental fashion, a Baroque extravaganza of devotion in which the virile Judas and the dismayed Peter are most prominent. For them Veronese reserved his finest tonal harmonies. The robes of Judas are a compound of silvery blue and golden brown and Venetian red, and these glittering tints enhance the colossal plasticity of his bronze-coloured shoulder, rising up rock-like before the whiteness of the cloth. In the twilight of the room the Apostles, leaning or bending forward in rhythmical movements, close the circle around the Christ, and they are performers of a rite rather than impersonators of an individual rôle. Veronese's *Last Supper* is a Venetian pageant, a continuous narrative, a sumptuous tapestry, painted in subdued and silvery tones, to decorate with its secular splendour the refectory of some religious house.

Throughout the second half of the sixteenth century, a Venetian master of the Counter Reformation developed the theme of the Last Supper with such variety and insistence on its magical character by a spectacular use of space and of light—Longhi's *scrittura di luci*—that his work offers a unique evidence of stylistic and religious transformations which took place during that period. Between 1547 and 1594

PLATE 59 TINTORETTO

Tintoretto painted at least six major versions of the subject for Venetian churches and religious societies. At San Trovaso all the elements of Baroque religion and pictorial vision can be seen, and the distance which the artist has moved from the classical organisation of space and figure-composition. The moment is the same as in Leonardo's *Cenacolo*, but the effect of Christ's words is diffused by the violent movement of the Apostles, the glaring restlessness of illumination, and the intrusion of the extraneous space in the depth of the picture. Though the Christ is in the centre of intersecting diagonals of figures, though the Apostles are not reduced to arabesques, but have substance and human personality, Tintoretto comes as a destroyer of the classical order and its contained religious solemnity. The mystical radiance that surrounds the Christ, the ecstatic fervour of the Apostles, their theatrical poses, their violent jerks express the effusive religion of the Church Militant, the southern intensity with which Ignatius Loyola exhorted his followers to experience in the mind's eye every moment of Christ's Passion.

By writing pictorial drama Tintoretto lent the most powerful aid to the form of religion that swept through southern Europe from the centres of the Counter Reformation. He conveys anxiety and disquiet of the coming Betrayal by the physical reaction of bodies, the violent contrasts of dark human silhouettes upon areas of dazzling light, and even by inanimate objects like the upturned chair. As four of the principals bend towards the Redeemer, and Peter approaches Christ with troubled, inquiring gesture, so others are drawn backwards in a centrifugal movement, and the Last Supper resolves into a scene of emotional fury.

PLATE 60 FEDERICO BAROCCI

No creative fury animates the style of Federico Barocci (1535–1612) who made the appealing sentiments and graceful poses of Correggio subservient to the ubiquitous religion of the Counter Reformation. His *Last Supper* at Urbino, in its pietistic suavity and florid elegance, foreshadows Tiepolo and the eighteenth-century graces, but in its rich and fluent handling of paint, its verve and movement impressed Rubens. It served Wölfflin as an example to demonstrate a stage in the dissolution by depth of the planimetrical style of Leonardo. For here the table is at the back of the room, where Christ breaks the bread and the Apostles re-echo the emotion of the hour; the foreground is left free in the centre, but from both sides intermediary figures lead into depth, a whole gamut of scullions and table lads in charming postures, like the half-nude Roman boy, taking the tin plates from a curly-haired child, who helps the dish-washer on the left. This diminishing scale recurs on the opposite side, where the cellar boy bends forward to seize his vessels and a pretty lad walks into the picture, gathering all the light upon his back. Angels hover in the upper air as so many shining lustres, invisibly suspended from the ceiling, and the outer world streams in through the open doors. Yet the lively "Rococo" world is subjected to a measure of symmetry: the two Apostles opposite Christ turn outwards and open the view to the centre. Barocci's *Last Supper* is a crowded, worldly scene, painted for the popular devotion, full of charming figures and incidents, an unashamed paganism, which blends so well with the emotional abandon and sense-enjoyment of the Catholic Revival.

PLATE 61 PETER PAUL RUBENS

With Rubens the Last Supper is not the drama of the *unum vestrum*, but the sacramental act of breaking and blessing the bread. Nearly in all respects the work of Rubens, which is of 1630–2, differs from its great predecessors. It is a night picture. The table is square, but the Apostles with glowing faces surround the Christ almost in full circle. Spatial depth is restricted, but the altar-recess with book and candles, the Baroque pillars and architrave thrusting into space, the twilight gloom of the church suggest bigness, expanse, mystery. All is concentrated upon the exalted leader, revealing the sacrament to a devoted circle of men. The subject of Rubens—as of Signorelli—is the Communion of the Apostles, the moment of their spiritual oneness. They have drawn closer to the Master than ever before; and as they behold the inspired face, listen to the miraculous words with dawning comprehension, loving and adoring, or obtuse and hardened, as Peter seems to devour the Master with his eyes, John leans upon His shoulders, so are they all, these rugged fishermen from Gennesaret, stirred or stunned by the inconceivable mystery before them.

Only Judas in his voluminous golden cloak turns his back to the light and averts his face from Christ: pondering, affrighted by his own thoughts, yet not the least noble of the apostolic band, with something of Michelangelo's *terribilità* in his dark eye and hair, the powerful neck and shoulder, strong enough to shake the earth in its foundations. Between these two poles, Christ's ecstasy, and the brooding strength and burning passion of Judas, the Apostles move and have their being, a contrast between immutable love and inexorable fate, which must take its course so that the Christian mystery be fulfilled.

As the Baroque transcends into Rococo and the complex of figures lightens, the loaded mass and dramatic pathos of Rubens are changed to the decorative designs of Ricci and Tiepolo. Again is the table spread out horizontally to assure a great central plane of light, again are the Apostles grouped on both sides and the parallels are enhanced by the architectural foil. To suggest recession in depth the artist of the Rococo did not need to place the table slantwise and to open infinite distances like Tintoretto. His magic was the light and the interplay of dazzling splendour with pools of shadow. The classical order, the symmetrical divisions are boldly abandoned and more painterly means are employed to free the centre. From the Apostles on the near side of the table with their accents of colour, saturated with light and set off by deep shadow, the eye is led inwards towards the Christ and absorbs the whole irregular group at a glance.

PLATE 62 SEBASTIANO RICCI

In the earlier picture by Sebastiano Ricci the space is more confined, more opaque; the two Apostles seen from the back and brilliantly lit, lean across the table, where Judas has risen, a stark, ominous shape, while Peter and John, sitting in the half-light with Christ, are turned towards Him. Baroque religion is never far from *theatrum sacrum* and the figures act their allotted part with dramatic verve.

PLATE 63 GIOVANNI BATTISTA TIEPOLO

Tiepolo dissolves all earthly gloom into aerial splendour and light. He frames his stage by four mighty columns and a backdrop of curtain, and behind it a radiant building with classical porch and sculptured figures. And here an exalted Christ, His arms spread wide like Leonardo's, His gaze raised to heaven, His head in an aura of light, eats the paschal lamb with His disciples. As the offering is made, the sacrifice revealed, Peter in his white priestly robe and flowing beard, like a prophet of old, looks upwards as if he beheld the heavenly host or heard the music of the spheres. The impact of Christ's words is strongest in the dark silhouette of Judas, drawn backwards as if struck by lightning, and it is in the contrast of these two figures, the exalted and the thunderstruck, that the tension of Tiepolo's melodrama resides.

# XIV. *The Agony in the Garden*

"*And they came to a place which was named Gethsemane, and he saith to his disciples, Sit ye here, while I shall pray. And he taketh with him Peter and James and John, and began to be sore amazed, and to be very heavy, And saith unto them, My soul is exceeding sorrowful unto death: tarry ye here, and watch. And he went forward a little, and fell on the ground, and prayed, that if it were possible, the hour might pass from him. And he said, Abba, father, all things are possible unto thee; take away this cup from me: Nevertheless not what I will, but what thou wilt. And he cometh, and findeth them sleeping, and saith unto Peter, Simon, sleepest thou? couldest not thou watch one hour? Watch ye and pray, lest ye enter into temptation. The spirit truly is ready, but the flesh is weak. And again he went away, and prayed, and spake the same words. And when he returned, he found them asleep again, (for their eyes were heavy) neither wist they what to answer him. And he cometh the third time, and saith unto them, Sleep on now, and take your rest: it is enough, the hour is come, behold, the Son of man is betrayed into the hands of sinners. Rise up, let us go, Lo, he that betrayeth me is at hand.*" (Mark xiv, 32–42)

PLATE 64
MOSAIC,
SIXTH CENTURY,
RAVENNA

After the Last Supper, Christ foretells the coming Denial of Peter and goes into the Mount of Olives to pray. In the mosaic at Sant' Apollinare Nuovo He stands high above His disciples in pathetic loneliness, His hands raised in prayer, but His arms clinging to His body, as He asks that the cup may pass. As the hills fan out on either side, with the writhing trees framing Christ motionless in the centre, a solemn shape, dark purple upon gold—so the Apostles beneath, wrapped in their white tunics and inclining their heads and bodies, are rhythmical groups of men in the grip of fear. The Ravenna mosaic is the earliest, the least dramatic, the least literal version of the subject. Peter and the sons of Zebedee are not separated from the rest of the disciples. Yet the mosaic moves by the contrast between the solitary agonised Christ and the sorrowing Apostles, scattered like lost sheep at the foot of the mount.

PLATE 65
MOSAIC,
TWELFTH
CENTURY,
PALERMO

The master of the medieval mosaic at Monreale Cathedral, in a design of concentrated power, compelled three scenes into one: the sleeping Apostles contained in the hollow of the circular rock; a tempestuous Christ exhorting Peter, and the Redeemer prostrate before the angel. The spiral-like convolutions of limbs and drapery are in the neo-Hellenistic tradition, and the artist presents the sleeping Apostles like a sea of humanity, a mass of limbs and billowing drapery in varied postures, an excess of spherical movement, of arched backs and sinuous swirling lines. Only Peter sits upright and transfixed, as he hears the sorrowing words: "Simon, sleepest thou? couldest not thou watch one hour?" Demus has noted in the Apostle on the extreme left the pose of an antique river god.

Strength and compactness of the Monreale mosaic and their Hellenistic flavour are transformed in San Marco, where the *Agony in the Garden* is drawn out in a long narrative frieze. Here an elongated Christ appears six times amidst the Gothic rocks with stylish plants and lineaments; and though the sleeping Apostles are fashioned in the Byzantine manner, the scene where a lofty and serene Christ admonishes Peter has a human warmth and poignancy which reflects Occidental art of the Trecento. For Peter kneels before Christ with such ardour of glance and gesture, like a soul in limbo longing to be raised to the heavenly sphere.

PLATE 66
DUCCIO DI
BUONINSEGNA

The dependence of Duccio's *Agony in the Garden* on the Monreale mosaic or some common prototype in Byzantine miniature is self-evident. Here is the same pattern of huddled men in studied poses of sleep, in a close semicircular build-up of bodies, though Duccio following a different Gospel has separated

Peter, James and John from the principal group. Moreover, like the mosaicist of San Marco, Duccio presents successive moments: the Prayer and the Exhortation. Medieval artists were not meticulous about the category of time. The mind's image was projected outwards, and the primitive viewer beholds at one glance Christ praying upon the rock and Christ admonishing the Apostles. The artist at Monreale accomplished this in symbolical shorthand; but Duccio brought to the task a new concept of space: a rising rock facet, punctuated by trees—dark green silhouettes upon gold—dividing, framing and heightening the action by a measure of realistic vision. For although these are stylish rocks and heraldic trees, by their recession and spacing they suggest the real earth, the Mount of Olives, and not the mosaicist's abstract cave, where the disciples are heaped together as in the hold of a ship.

The centre-piece of Duccio's panel is not the Prayer, but the Admonition, and here the three chosen Apostles, a bulky pyramid of weary men, "for their eyes were heavy", confront the Gothic slender Christ, a fragile shape, yet purposeful and expressive. For Duccio illustrates Biblical story by the simplest means, the Gospel which everyone knew and would henceforth see in just these moving suggestive forms of the old Sienese master.

PLATE 67
BARNA
DA SIENA

When Barna da Siena, working around 1350, painted scenes from Christ's Passion upon the right wall of the nave in San Gimignano Cathedral, he varied Duccio's arrangement and types according to the exigencies of painting alfresco upon large oblong fields. The Christ in prayer before the angel is still Duccio's meek and gentle Saviour, not without a touch of sentimentality. But Barna was a provincial artist, composing in large, simplified, almost rustic forms. He divided the scene in tiers or plateaux of brownish earth, where the Apostles are squatting as in an enchanted sleep, wrapped in their great mantles of pastel green or pink; and above, the selected three, heavy not only with sleep but with the credible weight of bodies, the gravity of their wide, generous cloaks, rose-coloured and gold. John in his troubled dream clasps the stem of the ornamental tree, and it is the luxuriance of southern growth, of laurel and olive and vine, which is the novelty of Barna's pictorial vision. For this is really a garden, not only a backdrop of big-leafed shrubs and feathery trees.

PLATE 68
ANDREA
VANNI

An illuminator's brush, dipped in heavenly hues, has fashioned Andrea Vanni's panel, which forms part of a tryptych of the Crucifixion. This fourteenth-century Sienese is perhaps not one of the greatest of his School, but he transmits Simone Martini's purity of vision, his singing colours and melodious flow of line, to a later age. But for the Byzantine mask of Peter, he has shed the inheritance of Duccio, and painted a pure fantasy of the chivalrous Middle Ages, complete with walled-in castle and knights, issuing from its nocturnal gate, and a radiant garden-prospect with flower-starred meadows and dainty trees—a miniaturist's vision of the Earthly Paradise, where Dante meets Matelda.

Like Fra Angelico da Fiesole, the masters of fourteenth- and fifteenth-century Siena painted their poetic dream of beauty, where the tragic or the evil had no place, and Vanni gave to Christ and to the sleeping Apostles such beauty of feature and raiment as his medievalist vision could conceive. The youthful John asleep between Christ and Peter, resting his fair head upon his hand, is more like Raphael's dreaming knight watched over by the antique virtues, while Peter clutches at the hand of Christ as if he were sinking in the water. Thus Vanni saw the Mount of Olives as a table-land of ornamental shrubs and flowers, where celestial spirits in human garb dwell and dream and pray in unruffled and everlasting beauty.

PLATE 69
ANDREA
MANTEGNA

There is hardly a link between the Gothic idealism practised in Siena around 1400 and the Roman grip on reality of the Paduan School only half a century later. But if the painters of Siena were romantic in spirit and reactionary in method, Mantegna was no less a romantic, if that term implies a nostalgic hankering after the past; for in all the Renaissance there is no more furious effort than his, to call back into life a Cæsarean spirit and a lost world of marmoreal form. Mantegna was hardly imbued with the Christian sentiment and his *Agony in the Garden*, unrivalled in compositional power and antique grandeur, is at the same time the least Christian. For the gigantic Christ who kneels upon layers of arid rock before a radiant vision of infant angels, bearing the instruments of his Passion—the winged

Cupids of Antiquity—is the darkest shape in the composition, and not unlike the towering rocks among which he moves. The Apostles lie motionless on the ground like fallen statues, their rigid limbs, their heavy breath, their deadly torpor suggested with stark realism. Mantegna was so possessed with the sculptural ideal that all his vital energy was spent on the bold modulation of plastic form, the foreshortening of bodies or the conveying of the relaxed and extended limbs of the Apostles in the crystalline space.

Bigness of human form also determines the scale of the landscape: the pyramidal rocks above an imaginary Jerusalem—an Italian hill city in the upper reaches of the Adige—its walls and square towers clinging to the side of the rocks. The topographical clarity of this mountain landscape is such that there is no pictorial transition between foreground and background. The sharply winding road and river lead the eye inwards towards a nimble group of legionaries who, led by Judas, issue from the city in search for Christ. Even the colours—moss-green, sky-blue and golden yellow—in this mountain world of granite and porphyry, serve to isolate rather than to fuse forms, and in the airless space cubic houses and rounded hills stand out in southern clarity under the azure sky.

The Paduan training of the young Bellini, his early dependence on Mantegna's genius are strongly felt in his contemporaneous *Agony in the Garden*, which translates the cyclopic work of the master into the gentler, more spiritual, more diaphanous art of Venice. The similarities and the changes are equally striking. Mantegna's concentrated compactness has yielded to a far looser, almost vacant design, and his overpowering figures are diminished in scale. Though Christ kneels on a central rock of primeval hugeness and the folds of His robe have the Paduan harshness and linear brittleness, His is a gentler figure, praying before a luminous angel in the sky, so much less disturbing than Mantegna's victorious cohort of antique genii. The Apostles too are more moderate, more human than the rustic giants of Mantegna, though Peter's foreshortened shape is a study in the Paduan style. But the troubled sleep of Bellini's John, leaning against the rock, and the natural poise of James, resting his head upon his arm, convey a religious mood, a spiritual state. For that is Bellini's own contribution to the art of Venice, as it frees itself from the Paduan tyranny, that intensity of feeling which flows over into the landscape and steeps the desert rocks and quarries into the luminous tints of dawn, lights up the radiant city and tops the dark hill ranges with a sea of flaming sky.

PLATE 70
GIOVANNI
BELLINI

The stillness, the poetry, the elegiac mood of Giovanni Bellini are swept away by the cries of anguish, the revolt almost of Holbein's *Christ in Agony*, his face distorted, his arms thrown up to heaven. This objective recorder of the human countenance began his artistic career as a Gothic expressionist, and in his early religious pictures he grafted his own ruthless realism upon elements of Grünewald's skies and landscapes. In his hands the Mount of Olives becomes a German pinewood, fantastically lit by torches and lanterns, with the spires of Basle Cathedral silhouetted against a cloud-ridden sky. And here the drama is at its height; for within a stone's throw of the despairing Saviour, whom no spiritual grace, no halo of sanctity distinguish from His pursuers, comes Judas, clutching the money-bag to his heart, arm in arm with a brutish soldier. For the young Holbein the painting of Christ's Passion was a task of historical narrative, without mystical undertones or innuendoes, his aim a strident veracity, free from all religious sentiment or human dignity. His Christ is a mortal man, maddened by fear, and Peter a besotted ancient, relaxed by sleep into a horrible grimace. Fierceness and intensity of the human drama are heightened by the closeness of large figures to the foreground, and there is small room to move in the constricted space; even the sky is eclipsed by the cup-bearing angel, foreshortened and seen *di sotto in sù*. Holbein's art, not yet ennobled by his later restraint, poise and immaculate form, reveals the German soul in the age of the Reformation, violent, dreamless and barbaric.

PLATE 71
Ascribed to
HANS HOLBEIN
THE YOUNGER

Realism in art may be defined as an unrelenting truthfulness to visual and psychological fact. At the other end of the pole are the abandoned poses of the idealisers and embellishers, which are sometimes accused of insincerity. If the young Holbein stands for an excessive veracity, Correggio, his contemporary, anticipates the sentimental religion of the eighteenth century.

PLATE 72
ANTONIO ALLEGRI DA CORREGGIO

Correggio's Christ, in His dazzling white robe and azure blue mantle, is seen in ecstatic converse with a graceful angel, whose raiment of Venetian red and gold, whose wings tipped with blue, whose soft, foreshortened limbs breathe comfort and bliss rather than religious solemnity. Nor is Christ's expression that of the stricken Lord, but of an exalted young prophet, whose eloquent hands and upturned eyes, whose radiant head and fair locks, falling gently upon his shoulders, convey rapture and exultation.

Correggio was a master of movement and light, and in the joyful angel, more Cupid than celestial messenger, and in Christ's floating posture, it is movement, the swiftness of the passing moment, which are represented. A pale dawn rises over the distant hills, lighting up here and there an amorphous shape in the dusky air of the middle distance, the sleeping Apostles, a barren trunk, a rocky mound. For Correggio was a landscape artist with a poetic feeling for woodland glades and fragrance, and though darkness wraps the disciples in symbolic night and enhances the solitary elevation of Christ with tragic splendour, there is a unity of mood, an utter harmony, investing landscape and figures with the same religious serenity.

PLATE 73
TINTORETTO

During the last quarter of the sixteenth century Tintoretto decorated the Scuola di San Rocco in Venice with a wealth of paintings from the Old and New Testaments, and in the Upper Hall, among scenes from the life and miracles of Christ, he painted an *Agony in the Garden*, which illustrates the turbulent fantasy and the refulgent pictorial manner of this artist. The novelty of such a composition does not only reside in the use of chiaroscuro, the shrill accents of light, which pick out shapes from the inky gloom of the surround, but in the incongruities of space, which subject the universe to the sovereign will of artistic vision. For Tintoretto's Gethsemane is a nocturnal thicket of writhing plants, where Christ lies embedded upon a rock, while from above a great fiery angel rushes towards Him with the cup. The organisation of space is of the boldest, for Christ comes to rest upon the phosphorescent leafage, and the ghostly train of soldiers, led by Judas, emerges from nowhere upon the sleeping Apostles. If the agonised Christ is like one of Michelangelo's Prophets, the virile angel, compact, foreshortened, swooping down in a wheel of fire, like inexorable fate, the Apostles, stretching their limbs in uneasy sleep, their great shapes moulded by long streaks of light, are remembered from Byzantine mosaics. Only Peter awakening, a recumbent rock-like silhouette, his bald head reflecting the light, connects the disciples with the approaching soldiers.

Tintoretto's Gethsemane is more spectacular than any rendering of the scene before El Greco by its magic shorthand of light, its grandiose gestures, its genius for decorative connotations, by which the drama of the Betrayal and the tragic discrepancy between Christ's Agony and the human indifference of His disciples are made apparent.

Before the century was out, religious painting was to be propelled by the dynamics of the Catholic Revival, the Spanish mystics and the feverish dreams of Ignatius Loyola into a realm of symbols and arabesques which uprooted the cherished conventions of representational art. El Greco translated into an abstract language of visual form the burning experience of his soul. In that he followed to the letter Loyola's precepts, to visualise in vivid spiritual imaginings all the stages of Christ's Passion. But he did not visualise in any known form of religious imagery. He created his own visions, his own scale of figures, his own substance and density of objects, his own movement, light, colour, and above all his own physiognomical shapes. These were a conglomeration of the Byzantine icons of Crete, seen through the prism of the Venetian palette and distorted by the trance-experience of the Spanish mystic. From it resulted the insubstantial, stage-like backdrops of his landscapes, the olive rocks and sulphurous clouds, the arbitrary perspective and the sovereign scale of supernatural shapes.

PLATE 74
EL GRECO

The essence of El Greco's *Agony in the Garden* is in such frantic visualisation, liberated from all optical laws, such concentrated pent-up emotion as can be no longer contained in static bodies. Hence his amorphous shapes and elongated bodies, his violent sweeps of draperies, rocks and clouds, his abnormal proportions and distortions of face and limb. The very rock assumes the flickering quality of flame, and clouds a rock-like density. Those swirling shapes in the ghostly moonlight enhance the spiritual agitation of Christ, a spirit in ecstasy, illuminated by a flash from above and shrouded in robes of opalescent reds and blues. In his uplifted eyes and trance-like expression one perceives the dark forebodings, and in his half-raised hands of spiritual grace the Agony, the passing weakness and the ultimate submission.

Christ and the cup-bearing angel in his golden robe are conceived in superhuman shape and dimension, while the Apostles in their embryonic postures, confined as in the Byzantine mosaic to a spherical hollow, are more like human pygmies. The life-giving religious emotion seizes upon the chief protagonists: Christ in ecstatic prayer, in mystical colloquy with God's angel above, and deserted by His followers below. The gigantic rock and spectacular clouds, inclining towards one another, form a substantial foil for the divine personages, while a distant hollow suffices for the sleeping Apostles and a moonswept bank for the token group of Christ's pursuers. "The melodramatic expression of a high-pitched religiosity" is matched by a poignant directness of rendering spiritual state in images such as no earthly eye has ever seen.

Giovanni Battista Tiepolo's *Agony in the Garden* is not only a spectacular, but a profoundly tragic composition. As a decorative artist in the lineage of Veronese, Tiepolo worshipped the light, and the novelty of his invention is in the blinding chasm of light by which he isolates Christ and the angel. Correggio and El Greco also surrounded the Saviour in an aura of light, but only Tiepolo conceived a cloud of fire "which suddenly rends the darkness of the night" and reveals the tragic vision of Christ, faltering in the arms of the angel.

PLATE 75
GIOVANNI BATTISTA TIEPOLO

The effusive religion of the south in mid-eighteenth century, tops, as it were, a millennium of traditional iconography, where Christ kneels in prayer on the Mount of Olives, with this radiant and rousing vision, this climacteric of religious fantasy: the Son of Man breaking down under the burden, not of the Cross, but of the anticipation of the Cross, Christ faint-hearted and fainting, but supported by the angel who, though he holds the Cup of the Passion, is an image of divine love and succour. By his presence the deification of Christ is revealed, and it is from this vision, which the disciples in their tormented sleep at the foot of the hill do not see, that the crowd of soldiers, fantastic legionaries and bearded Red Indians, swinging torches and tomahawks, are repelled. But in spite of this operatic holocaust of decorative stage-craft, Tiepolo liberated the theme from all conventions, and by his fascination with light and his heightened religious awareness, he gave to the Agony of Christ a new tragic momentum and radiant beauty.

# XV. *The Betrayal of Christ*

"*And immediately, while he yet spake, cometh Judas, one of the twelve, and with him a great multitude with swords and staves, from the chief Priests, and the Scribes, and the Elders. And he that betrayed him had given them a token, saying, Whomsoever I shall kiss, that same is he; take him, and lead him away safely. And as soon as he was come, he goeth straightway to him, and saith, Master, Master, and kissed him. And they laid their hands on him, and took him. And one of them that stood by, drew a sword, and smote a servant of the high Priest, and cut off his ear. And Jesus answered, and said unto them, Are ye come out as against a thief, with swords, and with staves to take me? I was daily with you in the Temple, teaching, and ye took me not: but the Scriptures must be fulfilled. And they all forsook him, and fled.*" (Mark xiv, 43–50)

PLATE 76
MOSAIC,
SIXTH CENTURY,
RAVENNA

The iconography of the *Betrayal of Christ* combines three scenes into one: the Kiss of Judas, the Capture of Christ, and Peter cutting the ear of Malchus. To this Duccio adds the Flight of the Apostles. The Ravenna mosaic omits the figure of Malchus. There, in Sant' Apollinare Nuovo, the Apostles stand fast and Peter draws the sword. Christ has stepped forward to endure the hurried embrace of Judas, and his movement, his shifty glance are contrasted with Christ's inscrutable calm. In his distant gaze from wide-open eyes lie foreknowledge and submission to fate. Three of the Apostles turn their heads away from the Betrayal, and by their anxious looks and movement, perhaps more than by actual space, they are separated from their Lord. Two Roman soldiers in red and blue tunics reach out for Christ with a simultaneous gesture. From their hostile group issues the attack, and as the Apostles avert their eyes in fear, so the soldiers gaze furiously upon Christ. Through the Roman stance of the ancient mosaic, where movement appears frozen and gestures are mere symbols, the drama of the Betrayal gains strength by the rhythm of grouping in the interval of space and the suggestive contours of neo-classical form.

PLATE 77
MOSAIC,
ELEVENTH
CENTURY,
DAPHNI

Five centuries later, the mid-Byzantine mosaic of Daphni evolves the Hellenistic prototype of the Betrayal as a scene in three actions. The Apostles are no longer there, only soldiers and Pharisees, surrounding Christ on both sides. Byzantine art reserved the profile position for the forces of evil, and Judas as he storms upon Christ, is shown in that way. He is a youthful Alexandrine type, and his slender form, his fluttering robes have a courtly elegance. Christ stands immutable in the centre, remote and scornful above the crowd, and does not lend His cheek to the traitor's kiss, nor does He seem aware of the soldier laying his hand upon His shoulder. By his loftiness of shape and of spirit the Daphni Christ, foiled by the large cross-nimbus, is isolated above his assailants. On his left, Peter cuts the ear of Malchus, a mere boy, who in defence clasps the Apostle's arm. Soldiers and Pharisees are the knights and counsellors of the Byzantine court, Malchus a page, and Christ the King, who in hieratic remoteness does not deign to resist the hands that seize Him.

PLATE 78
DUCCIO DI
BUONINSEGNA

The phalanx of men who stand in strict frontality to the left and right of Christ in the Daphni mosaic disport themselves with Eastern dignity and ceremoniousness. In Duccio's reredos of the Maestà, elders and halberdiers have veered around and beset the Christ in a menacing throng. The Byzantine mosaicist designed two groups of ministers and knights-at-arms in the act of a delicate political mission, Duccio composed an unruly crowd of irate Pharisees and ruffians, capturing an innocent man whom an odious spy designates with sinuous embrace. The emissaries of an Eastern potentate have become an Oriental rabble who have closed in upon their victim in a half-circle, their lances and torches criss-crossing the sky, their helmets filling the line of the horizon. As Judas wends his way snake-like to "entwine" the Lord, as hands and sticks are raised and the soldiers tear at Christ's robe, as an impetuous Peter attacks Malchus, the elders recoil at seeing the fortitude of Christ. The central tree exalts His calm and noble figure, as the great chasm of the diagonal hill accentuates the perturbed rush of the fleeing Apostles. Like no other medieval painter, Duccio enhances the drama by this contrast of conflicting movements: the serried ranks of men, punctuated by the vertical trees and lances, and the flinching Apostles, tearing away from the scene of disaster. The staid pattern of the mosaic has been transformed by the dynamics of space, movement and grouping, and by the emotive power of the Christian artist.

To illustrate the Gospel with moving comprehensible story, the Sienese painter devised a coherent flow over the whole decorative surface. Perhaps his figures rather skirt than tread the ground, hands do not grip and bodies lack the mass and the weight of Giotto's. The Florentine master conceived the Betrayal as an almost static event. Amidst the solemn approach of torch- and standard-bearers—as immutable a pattern of men and of emblems as those in Piero della Francesca's battle-piece at Arezzo—the Kiss of Judas is the magical centre of the composition. Vampire-like in his yellow cloak, a monumental shape, Judas envelops the Christ in its voluminous folds. He does not only embrace, he drowns, he absorbs, he usurps. His pursed lips, his aquiline nose, his hypnotic gaze are of the fanatic. He no longer "entwines"; it is with impetuous force that his bulk, his strength overshadow the slender unassailable Christ. For this vicious attack is countered by the steely endurance, the proud rejection, the sacramental intangibility of Christ. *Stanno di fronte il malvagio e il giusto*, as Professor Toesca wrote with lapidary simplicity: "the just and the evil confront each other, the one marked by his physical and moral stain, the other endowed with infinite sensibility which does not shrink, though it expresses reproof and bitterness".

PLATE 79 GIOTTO DI BONDONE

To the left of this main group a secondary action of hardly diminished power takes its course. Here a formidable Peter cuts the ear of Malchus with a wide, slashing movement, while a hooded pygmy of a soldier, mistaking him for Christ, seizes his cloak. Giotto has made this soldier unshapely, almost grotesque. Yet his hunched-up back and his outstretched arm are as suggestive of hostile strength as the broad sweep of Judas' mantle or the gesticulating priest in his purple robe. Giotto seizes upon one central theme with concentrated, almost physical power, presenting it in terms of volume and structural form.

In the middle of the Trecento, Barna da Siena was still close enough to Duccio's schemes to adopt certain types and actions of the older master. But Barna was of a different temper, and something had happened during the half-century to give to Sienese painting a fierce and tragic undertone. The plague had ravaged the countryside in 1348 and generated a preoccupation with death and with suffering and formed the moral climate to the last monumental epic of the Gothic, the *Triumph of Death* in the Campo Santo at Pisa.

PLATE 80 BARNA DA SIENA

In Barna's fresco at San Gimignano, a mass of brutal soldiers in steel-blue helmets is the foil for the Kiss of Judas. These murals were to impress the simple folk of the remote and many-towered hill city, and this accounts for the dramatic heightening of actions, an exaggeration of type, and the large planes of local colours. Barna's art is related to the Mystery Plays performed in church, crude and of violent simplification. The Christ in His luminous blue mantle and red robe is defenceless and meek, Judas with his hooked nose and leer is the devil incarnate, the soldiers are merciless monsters, and Peter in the foreground falls upon toppling Malchus with tempestuous force. Against the golden cloak of Peter is set the rose-pink of John, who anxiously looks over his shoulder as he quits the scene of physical violence.

There is something northern in the grimness and fury of Barna's types, a primitive contrast of good and evil, as drastic as that of Flemish Bouts who painted his night picture of the Betrayal a full century later. His Christ is marked by the meek ineffectual inwardness of pietistic religion. For Bouts preferred a dignified calm to excessive movement. His Apostles are the medieval Christians of the cloister,

PLATE 81 DIRK BOUTS

denying the body its due, impassive, gentle, sufferers not doers of things. Nor is the Judas who lays his head upon Christ's shoulder, and to whom the Saviour turns in sorrow, an abject or ignoble type; for Bouts was not conditioned to represent wickedness. This Judas is still a disciple—van der Goes might have painted him—his touch is gentle and his gaze without malice; he is bewildered, irresolute and unconvinced by his own deed. Christ suffers his embrace and lends His cheek to the kiss without reproof or disdain, with an utter submission to His fate. But it is the scene of Betrayal, and Bouts must needs paint Christ's captors, the turbaned officials and dandyish soldier who tugs at His robe, and Malchus down on his knee, whom Peter immolates. This must be the first night picture in northern art, with the clearly lit foreground group as violent as Bouts could make it, and the moonlit church and hill in the middle distance, from where the women are watching the scene.

PLATE 82 ERCOLE DEI ROBERTI

Ercole dei Roberti's predella to the Liverpool *Pietà*, painted in 1485, is like no other rendering of the Betrayal. Here battle is joined and the nearest analogy is that of the Lapithae and Centaurs, locked in deadly strife. Yet this is not an antique frieze, not classical art, no Pergamon and no Olympia. The cyclopic rocks and the fury of men, the nervous silhouettes against the sky, the stress and strain of interlacing limbs are the Ferrarese artist's calligraphic vision of a moment in Christian history: the clash of opposing forces on the eve of Golgotha, the rage of men out for the kill. As the haggard and ghostly soldiers pounce with spidery arms and knees upon their victims, as the noose is laid over the head of Christ like a halo, the onrush of men is halted and the sinister bulk of Judas attacks the Saviour with shameless embrace. The ruthless energy of the fight, the turmoil of battle are conveyed by this clash of conflicting movements. From both sides the fury of agile men converges arrow-like towards the centre, and this impact is repeated in the scene of Malchus. Are these the disciples in the midst of the fray, the youth in the clutches of the satyr-like nude, and the desperate man wringing his hands? For Roberti saw the Betrayal as the doomed fight of Christ's party against an exasperated and cunning foe, and with his mastery over bodily contours and movement, his nervous energy and violence, he presented the passion of the fight with that metallic incisiveness which was his chief vehicle of expression. In the Agony, which is like a sinister prelude to the Betrayal, he used Mantegna's idiom: the pathetic silhouette of Christ, solitary erect against the sky, and the Apostles' crumpled, inanimate shapes beneath the primeval rocks of Gethsemane.

# XVI. *The Denial of Peter*

"*And Jesus saith unto him, Verily I say unto thee, that this day, even in this night before the cock crow twice, thou shalt deny me thrice. But he spake the more vehemently, If I should die with thee, I will not deny thee in any wise. Likewise also said they all.*" (Mark xiv, 30–1)

"*And as Peter was beneath in the palace, there cometh one of the maids of the high Priest. And when she saw Peter warming himself, she looked upon him, and said, And thou also wast with Jesus of Nazareth. But he denied, saying, I know not, neither understand I what thou sayest. And he went out into the porch, and the cock crew. And a maid saw him again, and began to say to them that stood by, This is one of them. And he denied it again. And a little after, they that stood by said again to Peter, Surely thou art one of them: for thou art a Galilæan, and thy speech agreeth thereto. But he began to curse and to swear, saying, I know not this man of whom ye speak. And the second time the cock crew: and Peter called to mind the word that Jesus said unto him, Before the cock crow twice, thou shalt deny me thrice. And when he thought thereon, he wept.*" (Mark xiv, 66–72)

The Announcement of Peter's Denial is made after the Last Supper, when Jesus foresaw that his disciples would lack the strength to share or to witness his Passion. It is then that Peter's affection and limitation come to the fore: "Although all shall be offended, yet will not I." The rebuke and the prophecy which follow—really a literary context on the spiritual plane—are a rare subject in pictorial art. But in Sant' Apollinare Nuovo the two stages of the Denial are shown. In the first, the cock and his column separate Peter from Christ and his mysterious companion, who follows him like His shadow or prompts him like His spirit. The primitive symbolism of the mosaic projects into visual form the prophecy of Christ, while look and gesture make his words emphatic. Peter hears, but does not fathom the truth; he raises his finger to his forehead like a puzzled man. All this is expressed by the force of linear contour, the sparing language of hands, the rarefied colours of purple and white upon gold. In Peter's Denial the drama has been translated into movement. As the maid bends forward to accuse, so Peter retreats in defence. Inexorably she besets Peter who withdraws in confusion and terror, raising the palms of his hands in Oriental fashion. The mosaicist aims at monumental effect. The actors perform in the forecourt of a house which is no larger than themselves. All the tragedy is contained in the rhythmical and spatial relationship of these two figures.

PLATE 83 MOSAIC, SIXTH CENTURY, RAVENNA

PLATE 84 MOSAIC, SIXTH CENTURY, RAVENNA

The human protagonists in the Ravenna mosaic are like tragedians in the antique theatre. They seem to proclaim, to mime, almost to dance; their whole body is in action. Duccio paints a situation. Outside the palace of the High Priest Peter dallies with the elders over a fire. These bearded Orientals discuss the events of the day with grave and sullen concern, and Peter has taken up his post amongst them. They warm their hands over the embers and Peter his feet. Then the maidservant passes by with her kettle to go up the outer stairs of the house. In a flash of recognition she exclaims: "And thou also wast with Jesus of Nazareth." Her arm already on the landing, she points to Peter, who stoutly rejects the accusation. The elders look up sharply. The lie is ill-concealed.

PLATE 85 DUCCIO DI BUONINSEGNA

We see the servant only from the back, but the effect of her words upon Peter is striking. He is not aware that he is burning the soles of his feet; he stares bewildered, he raises a rigid hand, while the elders look about them with sinister disbelief. Duccio inscribes with the subtlety of the miniaturist the tension, the anguish of the moment, a psycho-physical situation. He imagines the scene with southern intensity, the forecourt of the house, the Byzantine group of ancients among whom Peter tries to hide his identity, the accident of the recognition. He motivates and narrates the sequence of events, as he perceives them, with clarity and with cunning, and he leaves the spectator in suspense as to the final outcome of the story. As an illustrator of sacred text he is masterful and in his age unrivalled.

PLATE 86
REMBRANDT
VAN RIJN

If Duccio indefatigably narrates, Rembrandt, after an interval of three hundred and fifty years, gave form to the depth, the pathos, the frailty of the human soul; and as in various guises this soul was his own, the richest in experience, the deepest in suffering, he reached a power of presentation, an almost physical force of expression which was the formal response to his tremendous vision. In the *Denial of Peter* he painted the suspense, the human agony of him who has made the great refusal. Only Rembrandt perceived the catharsis, the trial, the humiliation through which the Apostle must live in order to emerge purified and strengthened. The challenge which Christ foretold is made apparent in the rude physical presence of the maid and in the merciless light which lays bare the Apostle's soul. Others have illustrated Biblical story; Rembrandt alone delves beneath the surface of appearances and inscribes in a human form the workings of the mind: the strength, the wisdom, the saintliness, but also the fear, the shame, the Oriental cunning and the dialectics of his conscience. For at this hour, Christ, from the mysterious half-light of a room in the middle distance, looks back upon Peter, and this makes it appear as if conscience were knocking with ghostly insistence inside the adopted mask of the Apostle.

The emotional contents, the spiritual core of the picture, are made manifest by the incomparable density of painterly texture, by glittering loads of pigment, by sculptured forms carved out of surrounding darkness. The impact of light upon the coat of mail, now dazzling silver, now like old gold, is softened by the deep glowing red of the warrior's cloak. The glare of reflected light from the girl's candle upon the Apostle's white mantle is the revealing source of the drama. From the transparent silhouette of her accusing hand, from the light of her crimson bodice, tints of coppery red pervade the room, shrouding the powerful frame of the seated soldier, his helmet, his lance, his armour in the atmosphere of the furnace. In the glow of this furnace, between the iron-clad hostile world and the human and spiritual loyalties which call him from afar, the Apostle's tragic plight is made apparent.

# XVII. *Christ and the Disciples at Emmaus*

"*And behold, two of them went that same day to a village called Emmaus, which was from Jerusalem about threescore furlongs. And they talked together of all these things which had happened. And it came to pass, that while they communed together, and reasoned, Jesus himself drew near, and went with them. But their eyes were holden, that they should not know him.*

"*And beginning at Moses, and all the Prophets, he expounded unto them in all the Scriptures, the things concerning himself.*" (Luke xxiv, 13–16 and 27)

"*And they drew nigh unto the village, whither they went, and he made as though he would have gone further. But they constrained him, saying, Abide with us, for it is towards evening, and the day is far spent: And he went in, to tarry with them. And it came to pass, as he sat at meat with them, he took bread, and blessed it, and brake, and gave to them. And their eyes were opened, and they knew him, and he vanished out of their sight. And they said one unto another, Did not our heart burn within us, while he talked with us by the way, and while he opened to us the Scriptures?*" (Luke xxiv, 28–32)

PLATE 87
MOSAIC,
SIXTH CENTURY,
RAVENNA

The Walk to Emmaus does not admit a great variety of presentation. In mosaic art the three pilgrims walk into the picture facing the spectator, and the village lies behind them or at their side. In Ravenna the three figures are spread across the whole of the picture plane, and their hands more than their feet or bodies suggest movement and destination. Only one of the disciples strides out towards the left, where on a rocky mound a castellated building symbolises the town. The pilgrims do not recognise the Saviour in their midst; calmly and in thoughtful composure they proceed on their way, listening to Christ expounding the Scriptures, in harmony of spirit and of purpose. The Saviour, though not larger than His companions, is elevated above them, His head foiled by the great wheel of the halo.

At Monreale the quiet gait of the pilgrims has become a restless and agitated rush of elongated figures, with garments fluttering in the breeze and hands thrown up in the air. Christ does not walk in their midst, but at their side, with bare legs and shoulder, wrapped in a shroud, His right hand raised. A narrow Gothic gateway emphasises the verticality of the figures, who stride towards it in the nervous abruptness of their movement.

PLATE 88
DUCCIO DI
BUONINSEGNA

Duccio borrowed Christ's gesture of hand from Monreale and something of Ravenna's stolid Romanesque architecture. Christ walks behind the disciples who have halted at the city gate, and the younger of the two invites the Saviour with a graceful movement to enter there and tarry with them. For Duccio has chosen this moment of persuasion when the three pilgrims have reached the village and Christ "made as though he would have gone further. But they constrained him, saying, Abide with us for it is towards evening and the day is far spent."

They have left the sunny distances behind, and in front of them, large and inviting, looms the medieval city with cobbled pavement and hospitable roofs. Duccio follows the Byzantine pattern, but he has a changed concept of space and of human relationship. In Ravenna and Monreale the architecture is dwarfed by the scale of the human figures. But Duccio restores the natural proportion and order, and endows his pilgrims with spiritual grace. The disciples cannot yet be aware of Christ's identity, but they gaze upon Him in wonder.

PLATE 89
ALTOBELLO
MELONE

The walk of the two disciples along the road to Emmaus, and their encounter with Christ, is the text of a sixteenth-century painter from northern Italy, Altobello Melone of Cremona. Jesus has come upon them unawares. He has placed His hand lightly upon the disciple's shoulder and put His question. The two are startled by the stranger who professes not to know the events which fill their minds. In the older man's gesture, in his grave and saddened face, are reflected the sorrow, the heaviness of heart. The gait of the younger, as he steps lightly upon the ground, looking back over his shoulder, is more lithe, more elegant. In the middle distance the three pilgrims are seen again, walking towards the city.

The disciples are wrapped in heavy cloaks of cloth of gold which fall in weighty folds over their robes of pale blue and moss-green. Their gestures are sparing, their gait is processional. Christ with His pilgrim's hat and staff and short tunic is more shepherd than pilgrim. The figures, though over-large and detached rather than submerged in the landscape, are related to its salient features, the autumn foliage, the rustic buildings, the vague, Venetian distance under the blue and mottled sky of summer.

PLATE 90
TITIAN

In the 1540's Titian painted the *Supper at Emmaus*, and here the analogy of the disciple in the shadow, who draws sharply back, with that of Judas in Leonardo's *Last Supper* is very marked. Christ is blessing the bread, and the moment is represented when the disciples' "eyes were opened and they knew him". The mellow light of the end of day, the dusky air of the Venetian landscape without, determine the mood of the picture and the classical symmetry of the three figures at the table is made less apparent by the spacing of column and tree. A "vesperal mildness" emanates from the figure of Christ, intangible and remote, and the disciples are filled with the divinity of His presence. There are only two modes of expression, two spiritual states, apart from the servant's quite physical unconcern: the pious adoration of the disciple on the right whose communion with the Saviour is inward and absolute, and the dramatic brusqueness of His companion who draws back in awe. The boy with the dish belongs to the outer world and looks only at the major-domo. Christ upright and frontal is in the centre of the composition, the disciples at equal intervals from Him are in strict profile. The pilgrim's staff by the pillar repeats the diagonal poise of their bodies. The oblong table with the radiant cloth is splendidly appointed by rarefied detail of still-life, scattered with seeming unconcern, the flat bowl in the centre, the shining goblets, the loaves and the knife. But above all it is the painterly realisation, the composite tones of the Venetian palette which, in the graded light, clothe the Emmaus pilgrims with that distinctive humanity and spiritual beauty.

PLATE 91
PAOLO
VERONESE

Between Titian's aristocratic calm and the grandly decorative Emmaus picture by Veronese lies only a small interval of time. But stylistically it is the change from the classical mode of seeing and feeling to the mannerist, from the composure of an established spiritual order to the melodramatic emphasis of the Baroque. Veronese, in order to convey exaltation and holiness, gives to his Christ those upturned eyes, the radiance, the pious, soulful glance, where Titian portrayed distinction and sanctity of a superior being. A ray of Christ's ecstasy also falls upon the disciples who are drawn into His aura. But Veronese's disciples are two rustics who reflect the presence of the Resurrected Christ by their own agitation. They seem to shout, they gesticulate, they cannot contain themselves on their seats. And so are the auxiliary figures made to serve the same purpose, converging upon Christ, and by their looks, their movement, drawing us into the picture. The Christ in front of the central column, the disciples swinging around towards Him, the vacant spaces filled with accessory figures, even to the little rose-coloured girl with the pup in the foreground—as irrelevant as she is charming—form a vigorous compact group of firm plasticity and decorative splendour. Luxuriant colour is lavished upon vast areas of drapery, golden cloaks betwixt silky linen, euphonic chords of sparkling green, Venetian red and of blue. For Veronese's ecstatic religion does not run counter to worldly elegance, a feast for the senses, an exuberant joy of living.

PLATE 92
MICHELANGELO
MERISI DA
CARAVAGGIO

Religious feeling in Veronese had been frank, naïve and sentimental. In Caravaggio, half a century later, it became democratic. His *Supper at Emmaus* is a tavern scene, a brilliant painting of genre. His boyish Christ is a preaching adventurer or vagrant missionary, expounding a message to His companions. Caravaggio had come to destroy the heroic and classical modes of Renaissance painting. The heavenly aristocrats were dethroned and replaced by the ruffians of the Roman countryside. Religious subjects are exploited with ruthless veracity and disillusionment. *Supper at Emmaus* is first of all a marvellous still-life, where a roast chicken on a platter, the crisp chunks of bread, a fruit-basket, precariously poised at the edge of the table, and a majolica jug vie with Velazquez and the old Dutch masters.

The magic of Christ is invested in the light; light which blazes from an invisible source upon His brow, His smooth oval face, the beige-coloured mantle and crimson robe. Caravaggio's Saviour with His long ringlets framing His beardless face, the pointed chin, the moist lips, though He is in earnest, will not yield any religious emotion. His eloquent hands, His striking thrust into space, His downward glance are spectacular, like His shadow upon the wall, the chiaroscuro which modulates His shape. Nor are the disciples other than Roman menials who accompany the revelations of their youthful leader with extravagant gestures.

Caravaggio's famous realism does not reside only in the selection of type, but also in the *bravura* of his rendering their labourers' fists and faces, their huge palms and thumbs, the brilliantly contracted sleeve, the leather jerkin of the one, the olive-green doublet, split at the shoulder of the other. Nor is the Spanish innkeeper less favoured by rustic naturalism and tonal harmony. In Bernard Berenson's telling phrase Caravaggio's *Supper at Emmaus* represents "hard-visaged peasants, humping shoulders and arms shot out, who have heard something startling".

PLATE 93
PETER PAUL
RUBENS

Anti-classical elements in Caravaggio, besides the vulgarity of type and their physical unrestraint, are the diagonal composition and the violent accents of light. Rubens in one of his last and most poetical works, the Emmaus picture in the Prado, moves the principal figure out of the central axis and opens at the back an infinity of space, a diagonal recession in depth of architectural forms and rolling hills and sky. The unifying force which invests the picture with its sunset glow is the light; the light of the dying day which falls in through the portico from the left and illuminates the exalted Christ, who alone balances the group of three by dint of its spiritual and physical radiance. The magic of chiaroscuro and light, which Rubens shares with Caravaggio, has become the principal vehicle of the Baroque. But it is no longer the sudden accents of theatrical illumination, but rather the unifying flow of light which envelops figures and landscape with the same golden warmth of sunlit atmosphere, the conduct of its rays, rebounding from arm and neck of the disciple or playing upon stone pillar and vault and reserving its greatest emphasis for the radiant countenance of Christ.

Christ and the Apostles form a triangular group, and while the older man recoils in sudden awareness and recognition, the younger humbly raises his hat and bows to the Saviour, his arm extended towards the landscape. The fat innkeeper with his faun-like ears and double chin, a contrast to the grander human shapes at the table, also looks across to the Christ, so that the gaze of the three carries us back to the principal figure. But considerations of structural form hardly reflect the nature of the painting, its singular richness and subtlety of colour, its human warmth and constraint, its spiritual innuendoes, its sheer beauty. Among all renderings of the scene it is perhaps the ripest, the most direct, the most appealing.

PLATE 94
REMBRANDT
VAN RIJN

The mood of Rubens' *Supper at Emmaus* is akin to music, an elevation of the spirit in the figure of Christ and a reverential, a quite human devotion in the disciples. The mysticism, the effusion of love are Catholic, joyful, almost pagan, embracing not only man, but also the beauteous world without, the whole creation. Rembrandt's *Christ at Emmaus* is an emanation of the Protestant concept of religion. The severe, puritanical setting, the dark enormity of the barren stone wall, flanked by Baroque pilasters, where Christ sits at table, are as significant of the Protestant spirit as the northern gloom, the chiaroscuro, and the accents of sorrow and suffering inscribed in His countenance.

The picture has been inimitably described by Fromentin, and the elements that compose its compassionate nudity are few. The disciple on the left has folded his hands in a sudden flash of recognition.

His companion has put his napkin on the table and stares; in him we are made to witness the dawning knowledge. The servant who brings the dish is halted by seeing Christ breaking the bread. "Has He ever been imagined thus before—pale, emaciated, seated full-faced, breaking bread as He had done the night of the Last Supper, in His pilgrim's robe, with His blackish lips on which torture had left its trace, His great brown eyes, gentle, wide, dilated, and raised to heaven, with His cold halo—a sort of phosphorescence around Him which sets Him in a dim glory—and that something of a living, breathing man who has passed through death?"

Rembrandt has made visible "the intense ardour" of this "divine revenant", the unfathomable mystery of a tortured and resurrected God who, clothed in the garb of man and with the attributes of human suffering still upon him, transcends into the realm of the supernatural. Only an inward-looking Protestant artist of the north could conceive the otherness of the Resurrected Christ in an insubstantial, almost featureless vision of His spiritual body.

# XVIII. *Christ appearing to the Apostles and the Incredulity of Thomas*

"*Then the same day at evening, being the first day of the week, when the doors were shut where the disciples were assembled for fear of the Jews, came Jesus, and stood in the midst, and saith unto them, Peace be unto you. And when he had so said, he shewed unto them his hands and his side. Then were the disciples glad, when they saw the Lord.*

"*And after eight days, again his disciples were within, and Thomas with them: Then came Jesus, the doors being shut, and stood in the midst, and said, Peace be unto you. Then saith he to Thomas, Reach hither thy finger, and behold my hands, and reach hither thy hand, and thrust it into my side, and be not faithless, but believing. And Thomas answered, and said unto him, My Lord, and my God.*"
(John xx, 19–20 and 26–8)

PLATE 95
MOSAIC,
SIXTH CENTURY,
RAVENNA

In Sant' Apollinare Nuovo Christ's appearance to the Eleven is the last mosaic of the cycle where discipleship played so prominent a part. In it Thomas, doubting the reality of the Resurrection, is made to believe, and the divinity of Christ is established for all time among His followers. In this mosaic, Christ—other than in the scenes of the Passion—far surpasses the Apostles in stature. Hieratically He stands in the centre and raises His arm with a solemn gesture, revealing to the disciples the wound in His side and inviting Thomas to place his hand into it. The narrow, perpendicular doorway enhances the lofty shape of Christ, and the great circle of the halo lends cosmic significance to His head. The Apostles are more static than in previous scenes at Ravenna; only two at each side show surprise at the miracle, and Thomas bows low before the Saviour as a visible sign of his experience. The mosaicist has built his design upon geometrical form and upon the contrast between Christ's intangible aloofness and the wreath of Apostles below.

PLATE 96
MOSAIC,
ELEVENTH
CENTURY,
DAPHNI

In Ravenna Christ's action is that of the *Ecce Homo*, who reveals His wounds not only to Thomas but to all the world, and this gesture is strengthened by the pointing hand, the solemnity of His gaze, the gravity of expression. In the neo-Hellenistic mosaic at Daphni, Christ's attitude is more human, more benign, and He looks upon Thomas almost with compassion. Here all the figures are elongated and have an aulic suppleness and elegance. Christ stands on the step of the doorway, and Thomas approaches Him from below with a timid, fearful, reluctant gesture. The Apostles, Byzantine dignitaries of the court, whose slender shapes are enhanced by the long vertical folds of their tunics, stand by in attitudes of measured surprise, of watchful inquiry or staid confidence. The mid-Byzantine mosaicist transformed Christ's followers into a circle of faithful paladins around their king, and the Incredulity of Thomas into an act of courtly ritual.

PLATE 97
DUCCIO DI
BUONINSEGNA

Duccio's pace is quickened when he represents the Risen Christ. The bright reds and blues of His robe with the Byzantine radiation of gold are even more brilliant; His slender form more vigorous, more intense. As in the Monreale mosaic, He stands in front of the closed door facing the spectator, and while He opens His robe with one hand to reveal the wound, He raises the other to heaven with an imperious gesture. For this is not the meek, submissive Christ of the Agony in the Garden, but a victorious God, a Thunderer, who looks upon Thomas with sternness and almost a challenge. By a symmetrical arrangement of figures, where the Apostles converge upon Christ, Duccio has implied drama and action, not only in the sudden apparition of the Saviour, but also in the daring of Thomas and in the apprehensive Apostles who echo the event like an antique chorus. And as in antique drama there are also two leaders of the chorus: Peter on the left who lifts the palms of his hands in wonder and dismay, and John opposite who makes a compassionate gesture. Thomas is young and beardless and graceful, in a pale blue robe and lavender-coloured mantle.

Duccio—though he closely follows the pattern of the mosaic; though his Apostles are still the Byzantine ancients with set faces, curly beards and gleaming eyes; though their bodies show no weight under their colourful tunics and their feet suck but do not tread the ground—humanises and intensifies the Gospel stories far beyond the reach of Byzantine art. In him the courtly tradition of the mosaic assumes a dramatic persuasion, without shedding the sumptuous elegance of Byzantine illumination.

PLATE 98
CIMA DA
CONEGLIANO

At the turn of the fifteenth century the Incredulity of Thomas was a favourite subject of Cima da Conegliano, a Venetian master in the following of Giovanni Bellini and Antonello da Messina. His classical rendering is the great altarpiece painted in 1502 for the Confraternity of San Tommaso, and now in the National Gallery. Here the Apostles maintain a perfect equilibrium around the Christ who, a beautiful half-nude, wrapped in a white mantle, stands in classical *contrapposto*, showing His wounds. Thomas, a Judas-like figure, advances swiftly from the left and places his hand into Christ's wound. A heaviness of mood, a "melancholy sweetness" informs the picture, which by its fine grouping and by the distinctive humanity of the Apostles, by sensitive modelling and light, is a notable work of the Venetian Renaissance.

But it is because of its academic perfection that the London picture is outshone by Cima's masterpiece in the Venice Academy, where the three figures of Christ, Thomas and a holy bishop are seen against a pale blue sky and a mountain distance of greenish mistiness. Christ seems to guide and to restrain the sacrilegious hand of Thomas, who strides out savagely and gazes up with inquisitive glance, while the bishop looks on with sternness. Cima was not a dramatic artist, but, in this second rendering of the scene, he has struck a deep compassionate note by the contrast of the mild forbearing Christ, in the sunlit radiance of His flesh, and the dark bronze-coloured and impetuous Thomas. But Cima's inspiration was the air and the light which shrouds in mystery the Venetian countryside, and into it he composed his sacred personages, so firmly modelled with planes of radiant sunlight and deep shadows. It is by this harmony of sculptured figures with the transparency of his distances that Cima attained the power and the poise of his composition.

PLATE 99
PETER PAUL
RUBENS

A very similar arrangement as in the *Delivery of the Keys* was used by Rubens for the *Incredulity of Thomas*. The Baroque dispenses with the central position of the main figure, has other means of accent and equilibrium, and in the painting by Rubens the idealised beauty of Christ's body, its radiance, its supple modulations, its heightened reality, alone balances the group of three Apostles. Rubens perceived the miracle in the tangible lifelikeness of the Resurrected and did not aim at presenting a spiritual experience. His Flemish Christ in the lassitude of His posture, His swelling, breathing, muscular body, the great curving line of arm and shoulder, the generous fall of folds, the heroic stance of the whole figure, fills more than half of the picture-space.

Nor does Thomas lay his hands into Christ's wounds, but with transfixed gaze looks at the stigmata, while Peter, too, absorbs with his eyes the reality of Christ's presence, and John with a gentle, feeling gesture bends over the nail-wound in His hand. Rubens at the height of the Baroque confined the scene into a narrow, oblong panel, and by the direction of Christ's arm divided the space into almost equal halves. He allotted to Christ the radiant beauty of a heroic anatomy and placed the three disciples opposite, graded in depth, three modes of being and expression: one struggling to comprehend, one feeling and loving and one confirmed in his faith; and by the splendour of light, the tonal synthesis of scarlet, purple and blue, he clothed the group in a rich, sensuous harmony of form and colour.

PLATE 100
LUCA
SIGNORELLI

Signorelli's predella of the *Resurrected Christ appearing to His Disciples* completes the millennium of the cycle which the Ravenna mosaicist began in the sixth century and which found in Duccio its classical Italo-Byzantine solution. There the miracle of Christ, entering through closed doors, was stressed by the splendour of His apparition under the Romanesque arch, with the Apostles recoiling on either side. Signorelli illustrates the spiritual experience of the disciples, when "he shewed unto them his hands and his side". Christ is not clothed in the Imperial purple or the Byzantine gold, but in the shroud of the tomb, which envelops His martyred body in classical folds. It is the crucified God, the Man of Sorrows who appears to the Apostles, so that they may see His wounds and believe in the Resurrection.

Perhaps nowhere in Christian art has Christ's Passion been felt with such poignancy as in these small pictures of Signorelli's maturity. Here a nervous sensibility and a perfect command over rhythmical movement is joined to an utmost purity of the imaginative faculties. With such tempestuous gait would the Resurrected Christ step into the midst of His disciples, and this is how they would receive Him. Their compassionate movements express amazement and wonder, a whole scale of emotions from deep sorrow and contrition to cool, almost scientific interest in the nail-wounds of Christ. It wells up from the sides, from the two calm and upright figures towards the centre, where the emotive gestures gain in intensity. There is a secret correspondence between the figures, an infinite variety, and yet a firm grasp of form. The Apostles are arranged in depth, they converge towards Christ, and the three nearest are the most active, the most vibrant. In the small confines of the predella, Signorelli enclosed a wealth of movement, and the religious experience, which animates every figure, has been transformed by the act of artistic creation into visual image.

# Selected Bibliography


E. Diez and O. Demus. *Byzantine Mosaics in Greece. Hosios Lucas and Daphni* (Cambridge, Mass., 1931).
O. Demus. *The Norman Mosaics of Sicily* (London, 1949).
A. Grabar. *Byzantine Painting* (Geneva, 1953).
Ernest Ühli. *Die Mosaiken von Ravenna* (Basle, 1939).
R. von Marle. *Recherches sur l'iconographie de Giotto et de Duccio* (Strasbourg, 1920).
Emilio Cecchi. *Trecentisti Senesi* (Rome, 1936).
Enzo Carli. *La Pittura Senese* (Florence, 1955).
Emilio Cecchi. *Giotto* (Paris, 1938).
Pietro Toesca. *Il Trecento* (Turin, 1951).
Bernard Berenson. *The Italian Painters of the Renaissance* (London, 1952).
Bernard Berenson. *Aesthetics and History* (London, 1950).
Bernard Berenson. *Caravaggio* (London, 1953).
Roberto Longhi. *Viatico per Cinque Secoli di Pittura Veneziana* (Florence, 1946).
H. Wölfflin. *Classic Art* (London, 1952).
H. Wölfflin. *Principles of Art History* (London, 1932).
Max J. Friedlander. *Die Altniederländische Malerei* (Berlin, 1924–Leyden, 1934).
Georg Dehio. *Geschichte der Deutschen Kunst* (Leipzig, 1930).
Mario Salmi. *Masaccio* (Milan, 1947).
Rodolfo Pallucchini. *Giovanni Bellini. Catalogo della Mostra* (Venice, 1949).
Paul Ganz. *Holbein* (London, 1950).
H. Tietze. *Tintoretto* (London, 1949).
Antonio Morassi. *Tiepolo* (London, 1955).
Eugène Fromentin. *The Masters of Past Time* (London, 1948).
Jacob Burckhardt. *Recollections of Rubens* (London, 1949).
Emile Mâle. *L'Art Religieux après le Concile de Trente* (Paris, 1932).

PLATE I

(*S. Apollinare Nuovo, Ravenna*)

MOSAIC, SIXTH CENTURY
The Calling of Peter and Andrew

PLATE 2 *(National Gallery of Art, Washington, D.C.)*

DUCCIO DI BUONINSEGNA (Active 1278–1319)
The Calling of Peter and Andrew

PLATE 3 (*Baptistery, Padua*)

GIUSTO DE' MENABUOI (Active 1363/4–1387/91)
The Calling of Peter and Andrew

PLATE 4 (*Eremitani Church, Padua*)

ANDREA MANTEGNA (*c.* 1430–1506)
The Calling of James and John

PLATE 5 (*Sistine Chapel, Rome*)

DOMENICO GHIRLANDAIO (*c.* 1448–1494)
The Calling of Peter and Andrew

PLATE 6 (*Academy, Venice*)

MARCO BASAITI (Active 1496–1530)
The Calling of the Sons of Zebedee

PLATE 7 *(S. Luigi dei Francesi, Rome)*

MICHELANGELO MERISI DA CARAVAGGIO (1569–1610)
The Calling of Matthew

PLATE 8 (*Opera del Duomo, Siena*)

DUCCIO DI BUONINSEGNA (Active 1278–1319)
The Miraculous Draught of Fishes

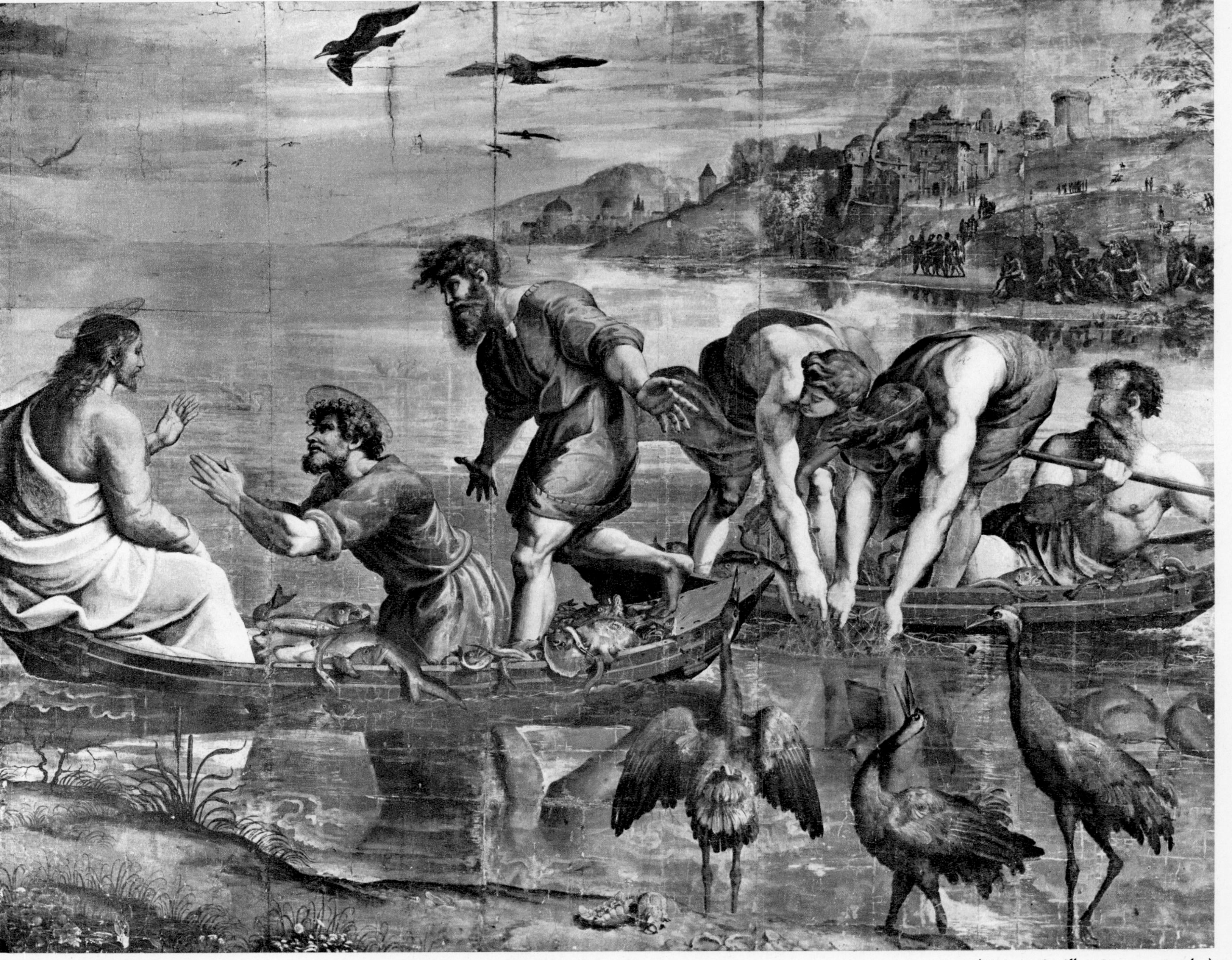

PLATE 9

(*Victoria & Albert Museum, London*)

RAPHAEL (RAFFAELLO SANTI) (1483–1520)

The Miraculous Draught of Fishes

PLATE 10

*(Church of Our Lady, Mecheln)*

PETER PAUL RUBENS (1577–1640)
The Miraculous Draught of Fishes

PLATE II

(*S. Apollinare Nuovo, Ravenna*)

MOSAIC, SIXTH CENTURY

The Marriage at Cana

PLATE 12 (*Scrovegni Chapel, Padua*)

GIOTTO DI BONDONE (1266 ?–1337)
The Marriage at Cana

PLATE 13 *(Baptistery, Padua)*

GIUSTO DE' MENABUOI (Active 1363/4–1387/91)

The Marriage at Cana

PLATE 14 (*Louvre, Paris*)

PAOLO VERONESE (1528–1588)
The Marriage at Cana

PLATE 15 (*Städtische Kunstsammlungen, Bamberg*)

A SOUTH GERMAN MASTER (Active 1485)
The Sending out of the Apostles

PLATE 16 (*Hampton Court Palace. Reproduced by gracious permission of Her Majesty The Queen*)

HANS HOLBEIN THE YOUNGER (1497–1543)
*Detail of Peter and John from* Noli Me Tangere

PLATE 17 (*S. Apollinare Nuovo, Ravenna*)

MOSAIC, SIXTH CENTURY
The Miracle of the Loaves and Fishes

PLATE 18

(*Church of the Carità, Sevilla*)

BARTOLOMÉ MURILLO (1617–1682)
The Miracle of the Loaves and Fishes

PLATE 19

(*National Gallery of Victoria, Melbourne*)

GIOVANNI BATTISTA PITTONI (1687–1767)
The Miracle of the Loaves and Fishes

LATE 20

(*Musée Rath, Geneva*)

KONRAD WITZ (Active 1418–1447)
Christ at the Sea of Galilee

PLATE 21 (*Uffizi, Florence*)

HANS VON KULMBACH (Died 1522)
Christ at the Sea of Galilee

PLATE 22 (*Samuel H. Kress Collection, National Gallery of Art, Washington, D.C.*)

TINTORETTO (JACOPO ROBUSTI) (1518–1594)
Christ at the Sea of Galilee

LATE 23 (*S. Apollinare Nuovo, Ravenna*)

MOSAIC, SIXTH CENTURY
The Healing of the Man born Blind

PLATE 24 (*National Gallery, London*)

DUCCIO DI BUONINSEGNA (Active 1278–1319)
The Healing of the Man born Blind

PLATE 25 (*Pinacoteca, Parma*)

EL GRECO (DOMENICO THEOTOCOPOULOS) (1545?–1614)
The Healing of the Man born Blind

T TIBI
DABO
CLAVE
REGNI
CELORV
ET QV
ODCV
QVE S
OLVERI
SVPT

PLATE 26 (*Correr Museum, Venice*)

LORENZO VENEZIANO (Active 1357–1372)
The Delivery of the Keys to Peter

PLATE 27

(*Sistine Chapel, Rome*)

PIETRO PERUGINO (1445?–1523?)
The Delivery of the Keys to Peter

PLATE 28

*(Victoria & Albert Museum, London)*

RAPHAEL (RAFFAELLO SANTI) (1483–1520)

Christ's Charge to Peter

PLATE 29 (*Wallace Collection, London*)

PETER PAUL RUBENS (1577–1640)
Christ's Charge to Peter

PLATE 30 *(Ashmolean Museum, Oxford)*

GIOVANNI BATTISTA PITTONI (1687–1767)
Christ handing the Keys to Peter

PLATE 31 (*National Gallery, London*)

DUCCIO DI BUONINSEGNA (Active 1278–1319)
The Transfiguration

PLATE 32 (*Museo di San Marco, Florence*)

FRA ANGELICO DA FIESOLE (1386?–1455)
The Transfiguration

**PLATE 33** *(Correr Museum, Venice)*

GIOVANNI BELLINI (Active 1459–1516)

The Transfiguration

PLATE 34 (*Museo Nazionale, Naples*)

GIOVANNI BELLINI (Active 1459–1516)
The Transfiguration

PLATE 35 *(Collegio del Cambio, Perugia)*

PIETRO PERUGINO (1445?–1523)
The Transfiguration

PLATE 36

*(Vatican Museum, Rome)*

RAPHAEL (RAFFAELLO SANTI) (1483–1520)

The Transfiguration (Detail)

PLATE 37 (*Carmine Church, Florence*)

MASACCIO (TOMMASO DI GIOVANNI) (1401–1428?)
The Tribute Money

PLATE 38 (*Palazzo Reale, Cappella Palatina, Palermo*)

MOSAIC, TWELFTH CENTURY
Christ and the Apostles entering Jerusalem

PLATE 39 *(Opera del Duomo, Siena)*

DUCCIO DI BUONINSEGNA (Active 1278–1319)
Christ and the Apostles entering Jerusalem

PLATE 40 (*Scrovegni Chapel, Padua*)

GIOTTO DI BONDONE (1266?–1337)
Christ and the Apostles entering Jerusalem

PLATE 41 (*Monreale Cathedral, Palermo*)

MOSAIC, TWELFTH CENTURY
Christ washing the feet of the Apostles

PLATE 42 (*Opera del Duomo, Siena*)

DUCCIO DI BUONINSEGNA (Active 1278–1319)
Christ washing the feet of the Apostles

PLATE 43 (*Scrovegni Chapel, Padua*)

GIOTTO DI BONDONE (1266?–1337)
Christ washing the feet of the Apostles

PLATE 44 (*Academy, Venice*)

GIOVANNI AGOSTINO DA LODI (*Pseudo*-BOCCACCINO) (*c.* 1500)
Christ washing the feet of the Apostles

PLATE 45

(*Wilton House, London. Courtesy: The Right Hon. the Earl of Pembroke*)

TINTORETTO (JACOPO ROBUSTI) (1518–1594)
Christ washing the feet of the Apostles

PLATE 46

(*S. Apollinare Nuovo, Ravenna*)

MOSAIC, SIXTH CENTURY
The Last Supper

PLATE 47 (*Opera del Duomo, Siena*)

DUCCIO DI BUONINSEGNA (Active 1278–1319)
The Last Supper

PLATE 48 (*Scrovegni Chapel, Padua*)

GIOTTO DI BONDONE (1266?–1337)
The Last Supper

PLATE 49 (*Lower Church of S. Francis, Assisi*)

Ascribed to PIETRO LORENZETTI (Active 1306–1348)
The Last Supper

PLATE 50 (*St. Peter's Church, Louvain*)

DIRK BOUTS (1400?–1475)
The Last Supper

PLATE 51

(*Ducal Palace, Urbino*)

JUSTUS VAN GHENT (1410–1475?)
The Last Supper

PLATE 52 (*Öffentliche Kunstsammlung, Basle*)

Ascribed to HANS HOLBEIN THE YOUNGER (1497–1543)
The Last Supper

PLATE 53 (*National Gallery, London*)

ERCOLE DEI ROBERTI (1450?–1496)
The Last Supper

PLATE 54

(*Museo di Sant' Apollonia, Florence*)

ANDREA DEL CASTAGNO (1423–1457)

The Last Supper

PLATE 55

(*Ognissanti, Florence*)

DOMENICO GHIRLANDAIO (*c.* 1448–1494)
The Last Supper

PLATE 56

(*S. Maria delle Grazie, Milan*)

LEONARDO DA VINCI (1452–1519)

The Last Supper

PLATE 57 (*Museo Diocesano, Cortona*)

LUCA SIGNORELLI (1441?–1523)
The Last Supper

PLATE 58

(*Brera, Milan*)

PAOLO VERONESE (1528–1588)
The Last Supper

PLATE 59 (*San Trovaso, Venice*)

TINTORETTO (JACOPO ROBUSTI) (1518–1594)
The Last Supper

PLATE 60 (*Cathedral, Urbino*)

FEDERICO BAROCCI (1535–1612)
The Last Supper

PLATE 61 (*Brera, Milan*)

PETER PAUL RUBENS (1577–1640)
The Last Supper

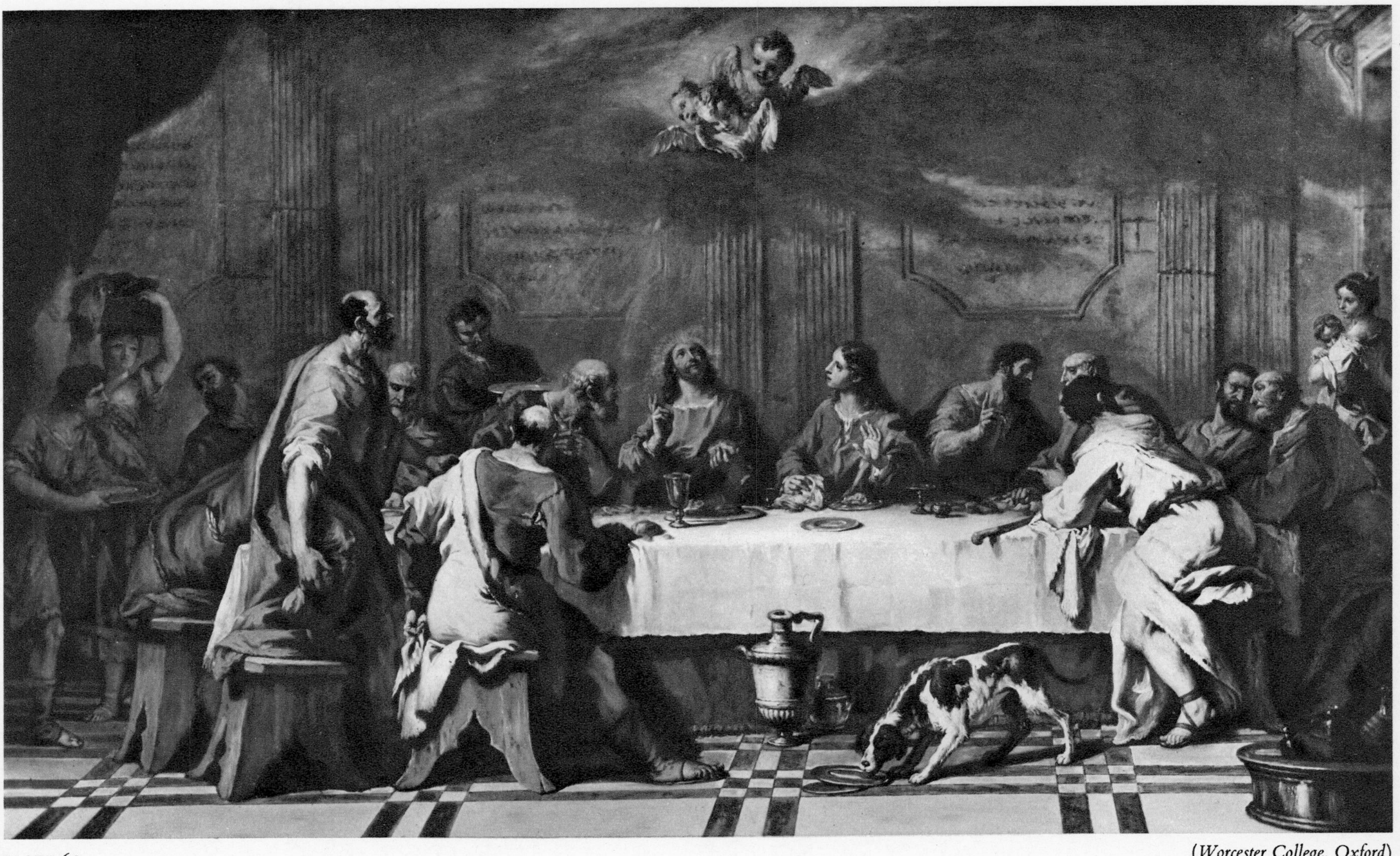

PLATE 62

(*Worcester College, Oxford*)

SEBASTIANO RICCI (1659–1734)

The Last Supper

PLATE 63 (*Louvre, Paris*)

GIOVANNI BATTISTA TIEPOLO (1696–1770)
The Last Supper

PLATE 64 (*S. Apollinare Nuovo, Ravenna*)

MOSAIC, SIXTH CENTURY
The Agony in the Garden

PLATE 65 (*Monreale Cathedral, Palermo*)

MOSAIC, TWELFTH CENTURY
The Agony in the Garden

PLATE 66

(*Opera del Duomo, Siena*)

DUCCIO DI BUONINSEGNA (Active 1278–1319)

The Agony in the Garden

PLATE 67 (*Cathedral, San Gimignano*)

BARNA DA SIENA (Active 1350–1370)
The Agony in the Garden

PLATE 68 (*Corcoran Gallery of Art, Washington, D.C.*)



ANDREA VANNI (Active 1353–1413)
The Agony in the Garden

PLATE 69

(*National Gallery, London*)

ANDREA MANTEGNA (1430?–1506)
The Agony in the Garden

PLATE 70

(*National Gallery, London*)

GIOVANNI BELLINI (Active 1459–1516)
The Agony in the Garden

PLATE 71 (*Öffentliche Kunstsammlung, Basle*)

Ascribed to HANS HOLBEIN THE YOUNGER (1497–1543)
The Agony in the Garden

**PLATE 72** *(Apsley House, London)*

ANTONIO ALLEGRI DA CORREGGIO (1494–1534)
The Agony in the Garden

PLATE 73 *(Scuola di San Rocco, Venice)*

TINTORETTO (JACOPO ROBUSTI) (1518–1594)
The Agony in the Garden

PLATE 74 (*National Gallery, London*)

EL GRECO (DOMENICO THEOTOCOPOULOS) (1545?–1614)
The Agony in the Garden

PLATE 75 (*Kunsthalle, Hamburg*)

GIOVANNI BATTISTA TIEPOLO (1696–1770)
The Agony in the Garden

PLATE 76 (*S. Apollinare Nuovo, Ravenna*)

MOSAIC, SIXTH CENTURY
The Betrayal of Christ

PLATE 77 (*Daphni Church*)

MOSAIC, ELEVENTH CENTURY
The Betrayal of Christ

PLATE 78

(*Opera del Duomo, Siena*)

DUCCIO DI BUONINSEGNA (Active 1278–1319)
The Betrayal of Christ

PLATE 79 (*Scrovegni Chapel, Padua*)

GIOTTO DI BONDONE (1266?–1337)
The Betrayal of Christ

**PLATE 80** *(Cathedral, San Gimignano)*

BARNA DA SIENA (Active 1350–1370)
The Betrayal of Christ

PLATE 81 (*Alte Pinakothek, Munich*)

DIRK BOUTS (1400–1475)
The Betrayal of Christ

PLATE 82

(*Gemälde Galerie, Dresden*)

ERCOLE DEI ROBERTI (1450?–1496)
The Betrayal of Christ

PLATE 83 (*S. Apollinare Nuovo, Ravenna*)

MOSAIC, SIXTH CENTURY
Jesus foretells the Denial of Peter

PLATE 84 (*S. Apollinare Nuovo, Ravenna*)

MOSAIC, SIXTH CENTURY
The Denial of Peter

PLATE 85

(*Opera del Duomo, Siena*)

DUCCIO DI BUONINSEGNA (Active 1278–1319)

The Denial of Peter

PLATE 86

(*Rijksmuseum, Amsterdam*)

REMBRANDT VAN RIJN (1606–1669)
The Denial of Peter

PLATE 87 (*S. Apollinare Nuovo, Ravenna*)

MOSAIC, SIXTH CENTURY
The Walk to Emmaus

PLATE 88 (*Opera del Duomo, Siena*)

DUCCIO DI BUONINSEGNA (Active 1278–1319)
The Walk to Emmaus

PLATE 89 (*National Gallery, London*)

ALTOBELLO MELONE (*c.* 1517)
The Walk to Emmaus

PLATE 90

(*Courtesy: The Right Hon. the Earl of Yarborough*)

TITIAN (TIZIANO VECELLIO) (1485?–1576)
Supper at Emmaus

PLATE 91 (*D. G. van Beuningen Collection*)

PAOLO VERONESE (1528–1588)
Supper at Emmaus

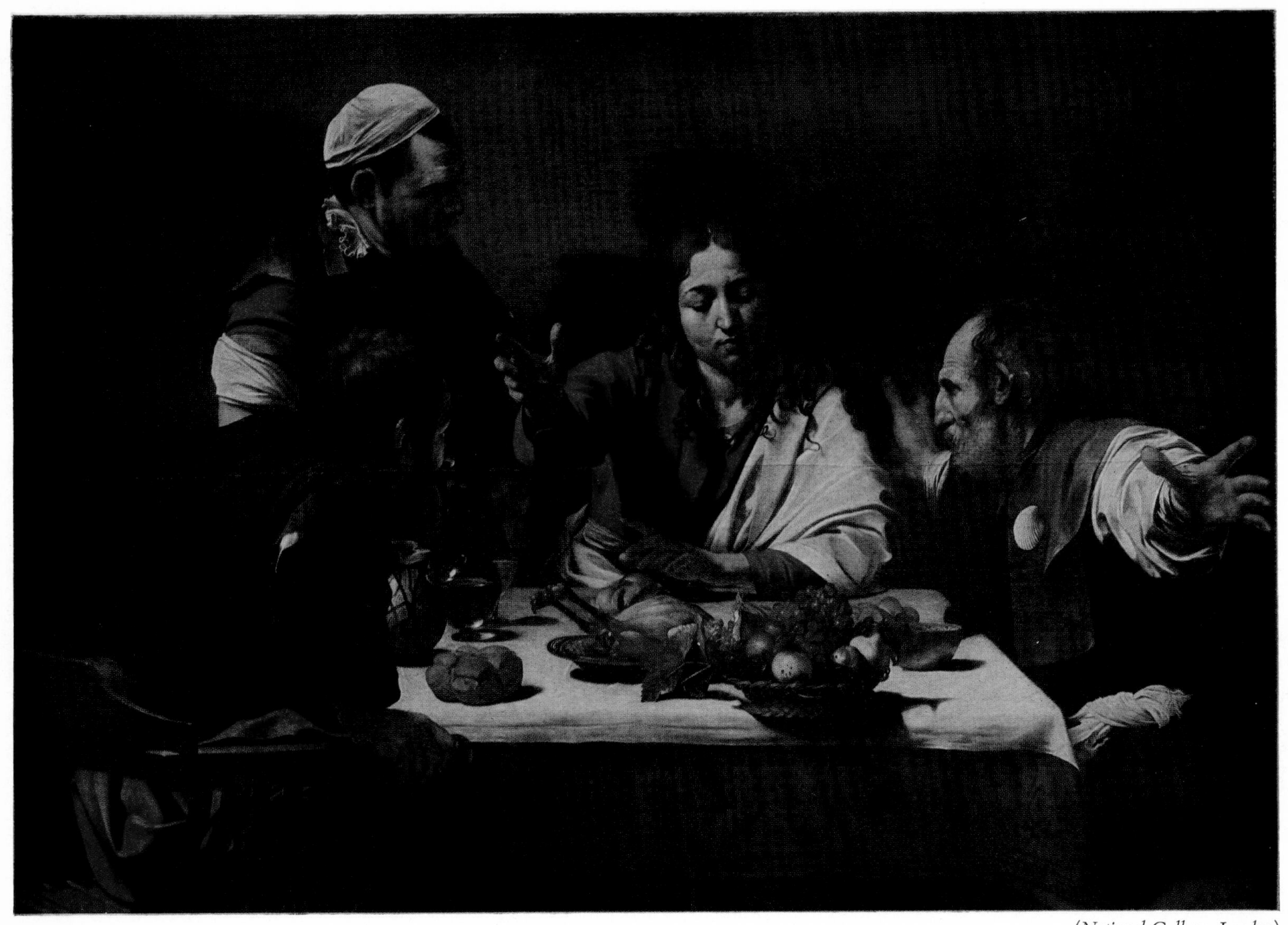

PLATE 92 (*National Gallery, London*)

MICHELANGELO MERISI DA CARAVAGGIO (1569–1610)
Supper at Emmaus

PLATE 93 (*Prado, Madrid*)

PETER PAUL RUBENS (1577–1640)
Supper at Emmaus

PLATE 94 (*Louvre, Paris*)

REMBRANDT VAN RIJN (1606–1669)
Christ at Emmaus

PLATE 95 (*S. Apollinare Nuovo, Ravenna*)

MOSAIC, SIXTH CENTURY
The Incredulity of Thomas

PLATE 96 (*Daphni Church*)

MOSAIC, ELEVENTH CENTURY
The Incredulity of Thomas

PLATE 97 (*Opera del Duomo, Siena*)

DUCCIO DI BUONINSEGNA (Active 1278–1319)
The Incredulity of Thomas

PLATE 98 *(National Gallery, London)*

CIMA DA CONEGLIANO (1459?–1518?)
The Incredulity of Thomas

PLATE 99 (*Musée Royale, Antwerp*)

PETER PAUL RUBENS (1577–1640)
The Incredulity of Thomas

PLATE 100

(*Institute of Arts, Detroit*)

LUCA SIGNORELLI (1441?–1523)
The Resurrected Christ appearing to His Disciples